Wisdom Sits in Places

Keith H. Basso

WISDOM SITS IN

PLACES

Landscape and Language
Among the Western Apache

University of New Mexico Press
Albuquerque

This book has won the 1996 Western States Book Award for Creative Nonfiction.
The Western States Book Awards are a project of the Western States Arts Federation.
The awards are supported by the National Endowment for the Arts and by
Crane Duplicating Services.

Library of Congress Cataloging-in-Publication Data
Basso, Keith H., 1940–
Wisdom sits in places: landscape and language among
the Western Apache/Keith H. Basso.

    p. cm.
Includes bibliographical references (p. 161) and index.
ISBN 0–8263–1723–5 (cl)   ISBN 0–8263–1724–3 (pa)
1. Western Apache language—Etymology—Names.
2. Western Apache language—Discourse analysis.
3. Names, Geographical—Arizona.
4. Names, Apache.
5. Apache philosophy.
6. Human geography—Arizona—Philosophy.
I. Title.
PM2583.B37   1996
497'.2—dc20   95–39272
CIP

Designed by Sue Niewiarowski

For the grandchildren of Cibecue,
and Gayle

Contents

Illustrations

Western Apache Pronunciation Guide

The Western Apache language contains four vowels:
a as in "father"
e as in "red"
i as in "police"
o as in "go" (varying toward *u* as in "to")

All four vowels can be pronounced short or long, depending on duration of sound. Vowel length is indicated typographically by double letters (e.g., *aa*).

Each of the vowels can be nasalized, which is indicated by a subscript hook under the vowel (e.g., *ą* and *ąą*). When one pronounces a nasalized vowel, air passes through the nasal passage so as to give the vowel a soft, slightly ringing sound.

The four Western Apache vowels can also be pronounced with high or low tone. High tone is indicated by an accent mark over the vowel (e.g., *á*), showing that the vowel is pronounced with a rising pitch. In certain instances, the consonant *ń* is also spoken with high tone.

Western Apache contains approximately thirty-one consonants and consonant clusters. Fifteen of them are pronounced approximately as in English: *b, ch, d, h, j, k, l, m, n, s, sh, t, w, y, z*.

Another consonant in Western Apache is the *glottal stop*. Indicated by the symbol ', the glottal stop can occur before and after all four vowels and after certain consonants and consonant clusters. Produced by closure of the glottis so as to momentarily halt air passing through the mouth, the glottal stop resembles the interruption of breath one hears between the two "ohs" in the English expression "oh-oh." The glottalized consonants and consonant clusters in Western Apache are *k', t', ch', tł', and ts'.*

Other consonants and consonant clusters are

dl as in the final syllable of "paddling"

dz as in the final sound of "adds"

g as in "get" (never as in "gentle")

gh similar to *g* but pronounced farther back in the mouth; this consonant often sounds like a guttural *w*

hw as in "what"

kw as in "quick"

ł This consonant, sometimes called the "silent *l,*" has no counterpart in English. The mouth is shaped for an *l* but the vocal cords are not used. The sound is made by expelling air from both sides of the tongue.

tł as in "Tlingit"

ts as in the final sound of "pots"

zh as in "azure"

Preface

What do people make of places? The question is as old as people and places themselves, as old as human attachments to portions of the earth. As old, perhaps, as the idea of home, of "our territory" as opposed to "their territory," of entire regions and local landscapes where groups of men and women have invested themselves (their thoughts, their values, their collective sensibilities) and to which they feel they belong. The question is as old as a strong sense of place—and the answer, if there is one, is every bit as complex.

Sense of place complex? We tend not to think so, mainly because our attachments to places, like the ease with which we usually sustain them, are unthinkingly taken for granted. As normally experienced, sense of place quite simply *is,* as natural and straightforward as our fondness for certain colors and culinary tastes, and the thought that it might be complicated, or even very interesting, seldom crosses our minds. Until, as sometimes happens, we are deprived of these attachments and find ourselves adrift, literally *dislocated,* in unfamiliar surroundings we do not comprehend and care for even less. On these unnerving occasions, sense of place may assert itself in pressing and powerful ways, and its often subtle components—as subtle, perhaps, as absent smells in the air or not enough visible sky—come surging into awareness. It is then we come to see that attachments to places may be nothing less than profound, and that when these attachments are threatened we may feel threatened as well. Places, we realize, are as much a part of us as we are part of them, and senses of place—yours, mine, and everyone else's—partake complexly of both.

And so, unavoidably, senses of place also partake of cultures, of shared bodies of "local knowledge" (the phrase is Clifford Geertz's) with which persons and whole communities render their places meaningful and endow them with social importance. Yet cultural anthropologists, some of whom work for years in communities where ties to place are vital and deep-seated, have not, until recently, had much to say about them (Rodman 1992). Places, to be sure, are frequently mentioned in anthropological texts ("The people of X . . .," "The hamlet of Y . . .," "The market-place at Z . . ."), but largely in passing, typically early on, and chiefly as a means of locating the texts themselves, grounding them, as it were, in settings around the world. And with that task accomplished the texts move ahead, with scarcely a backward glance, to take up other matters. Practicing ethnographers, much like everyone else, take senses of place for granted, and ethnographic studies exploring their cultural and social dimensions are in notably short supply. Human attachments to places, as various and diverse as the places to which they attach, remain, in their way, an enigma.

Some fifteen years ago, a weathered ethnographer-linguist with two decades of fieldwork in a village of Western Apaches already behind me, I stumbled onto places there (a curious way of speaking, I know, but that is just how it felt) and became aware of their considerable fascination for the people whose places they are. I had first gone to Cibecue (fig. 1) in the summer of 1959 as a nineteen-year-old college student.[1] I was captivated by Cibecue and almost everything about it, and in the years that followed, having completed graduate school, I wrote articles and monographs on such subjects as Apache ceremonial symbolism (1966), classificatory verb stems (1968), witchcraft beliefs (1969), patterns of silence in social interaction (1970), and a sardonic type of joking in which Apaches imitate whitemen (1979).[2] In between projects (no matter how captivated, you can't do anthropology all the time), I also learned to cowboy, camping and riding for weeks at a time with horsemen from Cibecue who were masters of the trade. In both anthropology and cowboying, I sometimes came up short, though not so much as to be wildly embarrassed, and when the essay on joking was done I began to look around for something new to do.

The answer came from Ronnie Lupe, chairman of the White Mountain Apache Tribe, a keenly intelligent man with a splendid gift for his own Apache language and an abiding interest in Cibecue, where he was born and raised. "Why don't you make maps over there," the chairman suggested firmly in his office at Whiteriver one day. "Not whitemen's maps, we've got plenty of them, but Apache maps with Apache places and names. We could use them. Find out something about how we know our country. You should have done this before." Mr. Lupe's suggestion (or was it a directive?) appealed to me at once, and a few days later, having discussed it at length with some of my friends in Cibecue, I informed him that I was prepared to begin. A year later, supported by a grant from the National Science Foundation, the project got under way.

Basically, the project had three parts: traveling with Apache consultants, many of whom were active or retired horsemen, to hundreds of named localities in the greater Cibecue region; talking with consultants, frequently at their homes, about places and place-names and the stories that lie behind them; and listening with a newly sensitized ear to how place-names get used in daily conversation by Apache men and women. The project continued for almost eighteen months, spread over five years (1979–1984), and this book is one of the results. It contains none of the maps we made (Chairman Lupe has determined that publishing these would be unwise), but places and place-names—and something of what Apaches make of both—is what it is mainly about.

"Mainly," I say, because Apache constructions of place reach deeply into other cultural spheres, including conceptions of wisdom, notions of morality, politeness and tact in forms of spoken discourse, and certain conventional ways of imagining and interpreting the Apache tribal past. For this and other reasons, the chapters of this book, all of which were written as independent essays, approach its central topic from somewhat different perspectives, offering as they do complementary "takes" on the significance of places in Apache thought and practice.[3] The reader will also find that each chapter is centered on a different Apache person, not only because he or she figured centrally in my work but also because senses of place, while always informed by bodies of local knowledge, are finally the possessions of particular individuals. People, not cultures, sense places, and I have tried to suggest that in Cibecue, as elsewhere, they do so in varying ways.

A book as short as this should not have taken so long to write. One of the reasons it did is that the experience of place—or, as Ronnie Lupe said, how people "know their country"—is, in anthropology and the social sciences generally, lightly charted territory.[4] There are few intellectual maps for ethnographers to follow, and therefore they are obliged to fashion them for themselves. But where does one turn for direction and helpful ideas? The answer, of course, is wherever one chooses to turn or, as Johnson remarked to Boswell, "wherever things look bright." I turned for brightness to an assortment of modern philosophers (Sartre, Heidegger, Nelson Goodman, Merleau-Ponty, Edward Casey), historians (L. P. Hartley, William David Chapman, Lowenthal), novelists and poets with a strong sense of place (Faulkner, Welty, Stegner, Cormac McCarthy, Larry McMurtry, T. S. Eliot, Heaney), writers on nature (Dillard, Ehrlich, Lopez, McPhee), a very perceptive physicist (Niels Bohr), and, since I was dealing with American Indians, to pertinent works by N. Scott Momaday, Vine Deloria, Jr., Leslie Silko, Alfonso Ortiz, and other Indian authors. I have drawn thankfully, though not always obviously, from all these sources and more, as I have from the incisive anthropology of Clifford Geertz (who continues to do it his way), the eccentric sociology of Erving Goffman (who emphatically did it his), and the sensitive sociolinguistics of Dell Hymes (who thrives on the complexities of Native American languages and likewise steers his own distinctive course).

Dudley Patterson, a Cibecue horseman, once said to me after a long day's ride searching for cattle in broken country, "Not many cows but many good places. Try to hold onto them. It's good. You could learn a lot." I did try, I have learned, and I hope that those who thrive on attachments to places will find value in this account of how others do the same. In this convulsive age of uprooted populations and extensive diasporas, holding onto places—and sensing fully the goodness contained therein—has become increasingly difficult, and in years to come, I expect, it may everywhere be regarded as a privilege and a gift. American Indians, who settled this continent first and were the first to be displaced, understand this already in very pervasive ways. May we all learn from them. And, as Western Apaches say in prayer and regular talk, "may it soon be usefully so."

And may I, on that graceful note, conclude by thanking some very generous people who shared their ideas on place with me and commented on my work: Vine Deloria, Jr., N. Scott Momaday, Jerry Flute, Gayle Potter-Basso, Karen Blu, Dan Frank, Michael Graves, Philip Greenfeld, Bill Douglas, Morris Foster, Edward Casey, Steven Feld, Nancy Munn, Alfonso Ortiz, Dell Hymes, Virginia Hymes, Richard Bauman, Joel Sherzer, Charles Frake, Roy D'Andrade, Harold Conklin, Clifford Geertz, Stephen Murray, James Kari, Eugene Hunn, Michael Silverstein, Thomas Thornton, Larry Evers, Katie Stewart, Miriam Kahn, Rachel Hadas, Sue Allen-Mills, Alan Wilson, Julie Kruikshank, William Hanks, Scott Rushforth, Peter Whitely, Jane Kepp, Ray McDermott, George Marcus, Stephen Tyler, the late Sir Edmund Leach, and Elizabeth Hadas, director of the University of New Mexico Press. The standard disclaimers apply.

Much of my fieldwork in Cibecue was made possible by grants from the National Science Foundation and the Wenner-Gren Foundation for Anthropological Research; I am grateful to these organizations for their confidence and support. I would also like to acknowledge the American Anthropological Association for permission to make use of previously published material. June-el Piper prepared the final manuscript with grace, expertise, and many helpful suggestions. Finally, I wish to thank the University of New Mexico for granting me a sabbatical leave in order to finish this book, and my colleagues in the Department of Anthropology for respecting it so cheerfully.

My debt to the Apache people of Cibecue, which now reaches back more than thirty-five years, is enormous and profound. No one could ask for better teachers or finer friends than horsemen Morley Cromwell, Charles Henry, Robert Machuse, Nick Thompson, and Dudley Patterson. Although all are with their ancestors now, I know they are still on hand, for I hear their voices often as I travel through their country. How *deeply* they loved their country. And how pleased they were that some of their knowledge of it would be preserved and made public, subject to a set of clearly defined restrictions which have not—and shall never be—violated. At their urging and with their permission, this book is theirs, a gift from them to the grandchildren of Cibecue, and to their grandchildren, and to theirs.

Other Apache people who have taken time to instruct me and show me how to behave include Lola Machuse (to whom I am particularly grateful), Ruth Patterson, Annie Peaches, Dick Cooley, Calvert and Darlene Tessay, Esther Lupe, Rose Thompson, Ernest Murphy, Joe Case, Sam and Lillian Johnson, Charles Cromwell, Sam Endfield, Levi Dehose, Lonnie Dehose, Francis and Sarah Dehose, Nelson Lupe, Sr., Roy and Nannie Quay, Teddy Peaches, Alvin Quay, Ervin Quay, Imogene Quay, Emily Quay, Simon and Beverly Endfield, Virgil and Judy Dehose, Delmar Boni, Vincent Randall, Ned Anderson, Philip Cassadore, Ola Cassadore Davis, Marlow Cassadore, and Franklin Stanley. I am also indebted to Nashley Tessay, Sr., who helped me no end in translating the stories and place-names which appear in the pages to follow. Ronnie Lupe, chairman of the White Mountain Apache Tribe for more than twenty years, has been constant in his encouragement, guidance, and advice. Working with him, as with everyone else, has been an honor and a privilege. I am also thankful for my friendship with Wayne and Flora Cole.

My mother, Etolia S. Basso, has helped in many ways. My wife, Gayle Potter-Basso, has helped in many more. Her resilient heart and critical mind saw this project through, especially on those occasions when my spirits headed south. To Gayle, with love, and to W., "Now it's pretty good 'aał."

Keith H. Basso
Heber, Arizona, 1995

Wisdom Sits in Places

Quoting the Ancestors

Place is the first of all beings, since everything that exists is in a place and cannot exist without a place.
—*Archytas, as cited by Simplicius,* Commentary on Aristotle's Categories

If, as L. P. Hartley (1956:1) proposed, "the past is a foreign country"—"they do things differently there," he added to make the point—it is everywhere a land that attracts its share of visitors. And understandably so. Passage to the past is easy to come by (any reminder of bygone times can serve to launch an excursion), getting there is quick and efficient (a quiet moment or two is usually sufficient to make the transition), and restrictions on local travel are virtually nonexistent (memory and imagination, the most intimate and inventive of traveling companions, always see to that). And however the trip unfolds, one can proceed at an undemanding pace, exploring sites of special interest or moving about from place to place without feeling harried or rushed. Which may account for the fact that returning abruptly to the country of the present, where things are apt to be rushed enough, is often somewhat jarring.

Just where one ventures in the country of the past sometimes depends on where one has ventured before, on personal predilections, nurtured over time, for congenial pieces of experiential terrain: the terrain of one's youth, perhaps, or of where one's forebears lived, or of decisive events that altered the course of history; the possibilities are endless. Yet whatever these preferences are, and no matter how often indulged, the past has a way of luring curious travelers off the beaten track. It is, after all, a country conducive to wandering, with plenty of unmarked roads, unexpected vistas, and unforeseen occurrences. Informative discoveries,

3

pleasurable and otherwise, are not at all uncommon. Which is why it can seem, as William Chapman (1979:46) has written, that "the past is at its best when it takes us to places that counsel and instruct, that show us who we are by showing us where we have been, that remind us of our connections to *what happened here*" (italics in the original). And why it is as well, for the same set of reasons, that this ever-changing landscape of the active heart and mind rewards repeated visits. For wherever one journeys in the country of the past, instructive places abound.

Many of these places are also encountered in the country of the present as material objects and areas, naturally formed or built, whose myriad local arrangements make up the landscapes of everyday life. But here, *now,* in the ongoing world of current concerns and projects, they are not apprehended as reminders of the past. Instead, when accorded attention at all, places are perceived in terms of their outward aspects—as being, on their manifest surfaces, the familiar places they are—and unless something happens to dislodge these perceptions they are left, as it were, to their own enduring devices. But then something *does* happen. Perhaps one spots a freshly fallen tree, or a bit of flaking paint, or a house where none has stood before—any disturbance, large or small, that inscribes the passage of time—and a place presents itself as bearing on prior events. And at that precise moment, when ordinary perceptions begin to loosen their hold, a border has been crossed and the country starts to change. Awareness has shifted its footing, and the character of the place, now transfigured by thoughts of an earlier day, swiftly takes on a new and foreign look.

Consider in this regard the remarks of Niels Bohr, the great theoretical physicist, while speaking in June of 1924 with Werner Heisenberg at Kronberg Castle in Denmark, Bohr's beloved homeland.[1]

> Isn't it strange how this castle changes as soon as one imagines that Hamlet lived here? As scientists we believe that a castle consists only of stones, and admire the way the architect put them together. The stone, the green roof with its patina, the wood carvings in the church, constitute the whole castle. None of this should be changed by the fact that Hamlet lived here, and yet it is changed completely. Suddenly the walls and ramparts speak a different language. The courtyard becomes

an entire world, a dark corner reminds us of the darkness of the human soul, we hear Hamlet's "To be or not to be." Yet all we really know is that his name appears in a thirteenth-century chronicle. No one can prove he really lived here. But everyone knows the questions Shakespeare had him ask, the human depths he was made to reveal, and so he too had to be found in a place on earth, here in Kronberg. And once we know that, Kronberg becomes a quite different castle for us. (quoted in Bruner 1986:45)

Thus, by one insightful account, does the country of the past transform and supplant the country of the present. That certain localities prompt such transformations, evoking as they do entire worlds of meaning, is not, as Niels Bohr recognized, a small or uninteresting truth. Neither is the fact, which he also appreciated, that this type of retrospective world-building—let us call it *place-making*—does not require special sensibilities or cultivated skills.[2] It is a common response to common curiosities—what happened here? who was involved? what was it like? why should it matter?—and anyone can be a place-maker who has the inclination. And every so often, more or less spontaneously, alone or with others, with varying degrees of interest and enthusiasm, almost everyone does make places. As roundly ubiquitous as it is seemingly unremarkable, place-making is a universal tool of the historical imagination. And in some societies at least, if not in the great majority, it is surely among the most basic tools of all.

Prevalent though it is, this type of world-building is never entirely simple. On the contrary, a modest body of evidence suggests that place-making involves multiple acts of remembering and imagining which inform each other in complex ways (Casey 1976, 1987). It is clear, however, that remembering often provides a basis for imagining. What is remembered about a particular place—including, prominently, verbal and visual accounts of what has transpired there—guides and constrains how it will be imagined by delimiting a field of workable possibilities. These possibilities are then exploited by acts of conjecture and speculation which build upon them and go beyond them to create possibilities of a new and original sort, thus producing a fresh and expanded picture of how things might have been. Essentially, then, instances of place-making consist in an adventitious fleshing out of historical material that culminates in a posited state of affairs, a particular universe of objects and events—in short, a *place-world*—wherein portions of the past are brought into being.[3]

When Niels Bohr went with Heisenberg to visit Kronberg Castle, he thought instantly of Hamlet and recalled the famous play in which this figure comes to life. Then, seizing on possibilities inherent in Shakespeare's drama, Bohr went on to imagine a darkly compelling place-world in which the walls of the castle echoed an alien tongue, a shaded courtyard nook gave notice of the troubled human soul, and Hamlet uttered his anguished cry, "To be or not to be." And probably, considering it was Bohr, there was much more besides: other fancied elements, wrought in compatible terms, which endowed his somber place-world with added substance and depth. Within this foreign universe Bohr could briefly dwell, and until it started to fade, as every place-world must, the imaginative Danish physicist and a bit of Danish history breathed life into each other.

But there is more to making place-worlds than living local history in a localized kind of way. In addition, place-making is a way of constructing history itself, of inventing it, of fashioning novel versions of "what happened here." For every developed place-world manifests itself as a possible state of affairs, and whenever these constructions are accepted by other people as credible and convincing—or plausible and provocative, or arresting and intriguing—they enrich the common stock on which everyone can draw to muse on past events, interpret their significance, and imagine them anew. Building and sharing place-worlds, in other words, is not only a means of reviving former times but also of *revising* them, a means of exploring not merely how things might have been but also how, just possibly, they might have been different from what others have supposed. Augmenting and enhancing conceptions of the past, innovative place-worlds change these conceptions as well.

By way of illustration, and returning once more to Denmark, Bohr's remarks to Heisenberg could have provided Heisenberg with novel possibilities for building his own version of Hamlet's castle in Hamlet's time, a place-world that would have been different from any he might have fashioned working by himself. And if Heisenberg had then returned the favor, describing in some detail his own construction to Bohr, the same would be true in reverse. Which is simply to say that discussing the stuff of place-worlds—comparing their contents, pursuing their implications, assessing their strengths and weaknesses—is a regular social process, as common and straightforward as it is sometimes highly inventive.

In this discursive fashion, even in societies where writing and other devices for "preserving the past" are absent or devalued, historical knowledge is produced and reproduced. And in this manner too, even in societies which lack the services of revisionary historians, historical understandings are altered and recast. It is well to keep in mind that interpreting the past can be readily accomplished—and is every day—without recourse to documentary archives, photographic files, and early sound recordings. It cannot be accomplished, readily or otherwise, without recourse to places and the place-worlds they engender. Long before the advent of literacy, to say nothing of "history" as an academic discipline, places served humankind as durable symbols of distant events and as indispensable aids for remembering and imagining them—and this convenient arrangement, ancient but not outmoded, is with us still today. In modern landscapes everywhere, people persist in asking, "What happened here?" The answers they supply, though perhaps distinctly foreign, should not be taken lightly, for what people make of their places is closely connected to what they make of themselves as members of society and inhabitants of the earth, and while the two activities may be separable in principle, they are deeply joined in practice. If place-making is a way of constructing the past, a venerable means of *doing* human history, it is also a way of constructing social traditions and, in the process, personal and social identities. We *are,* in a sense, the place-worlds we imagine.

But these and related matters are only broadly discerned and loosely understood, and the main reason why is easy to identify. A widespread form of imaginative activity, place-making is also a form of *cultural* activity, and so, as any anthropologist will tell you, it can be grasped only in relation to the ideas and practices with which it is accomplished. And because these ideas and practices may vary considerably both within and among particular social groups, the nature of the activity can be understood only by means of sustained ethnography. Yet little ethnography of place-making has in fact been undertaken, and what is known about place-making—Navajo or Norwegian, Sinhalese or Soviet, Mexican or Moroccan—is therefore sharply limited. There is work to be done, and now is as good a time as any to see what it may involve.

This chapter, which offers an example of the work I have in mind, is soon to cross over the border into an American Indian version of Hartley's foreign land. The time has come to travel, first to Arizona and the village of Cibecue, home since the beginning to groups of men and women known to themselves as *ndee* (people), to others as Western Apache (fig. 1).[4] And then to some of their places not far away—places with names such as Widows Pause For Breath, She Carries Her Brother On Her Back, and Bitter Agave Plain—places made memorable, and infinitely imaginable, by events that happened long ago when the people's distant ancestors were settling into the country. So let us be off, stopping here and there with one Charles Henry, age sixty or thereabouts, skilled herbalist, devoted uncle, and veteran maker of place-worlds. Niels Bohr, I like to think, would have enjoyed his company. For both men understood, though in very different ways, that castles come in a great many shapes and need not be wrought with mortar and stone.

Water Lies With Mud In An Open Container

Early morning, late May 1979, the night's redemptive chill rapidly receding before the rising sun. Silence deep and full, a blanket upon the land. I am standing with Charles Henry and one of his cousins, Morley Cromwell, at the edge of a circular swale some forty feet across. Ringed by willows and filled with luxuriant grass, it lies near a spring-fed creek which flows southeast to the gardens and cornfields of Cibecue. The earth at our feet is marked with the tracks of deer, and from high in a cottonwood tree comes the liquid call of a raven. A chipmunk creeps to the swale, secures a nervous drink, and darts away behind a rotting log covered with patches of green and orange moss. The air is heavy and moist. A small white butterfly dances in place in a shaft of golden sunlight.

Charles and Morley have brought me here at the outset of a long-range project in Western Apache cultural geography. Authorized and endorsed by the White Mountain Apache Tribal Council, the project's main objective is to record on topographic maps the approximate location of each and every place that bears an Apache name within a twenty-

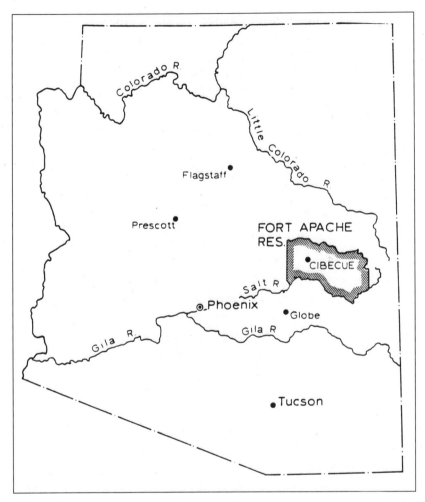

Figure 1 *Location of the community of Cibecue on the Fort Apache Indian Reservation, Arizona.*

mile radius of the Cibecue community. Residents of the community have never known maps they considered their own (those in their possession show but a handful of places with extraneous names in English and Spanish), and the work we have started, which is intended to lay the foundation for a local Apache atlas, is regarded by some as long overdue. A couple of weeks ago, before the work began, the three of us agreed on a simple division of labor. Charles, who is in charge, will guide us from place to place, supply each place's proper name, and comment as he chooses on its past and present significance. Morley will translate as necessary (Charles speaks English reluctantly, and my own Apache is stiff and uneven at best) and offer additional insights. My job is to drive the Jeep, provide plenty of coffee and Reese's Peanut Butter Cups (Morley has a serious weakness for them), and try to get everything down on paper and audiotapes. It seems like a sensible plan, balanced and loosely efficient, and all of us believe it will serve our purpose well.

But already, on only our second day in the country together, a problem has come up. For the third time in as many tries, I have mispronounced the Apache name of the boggy swale before us, and Charles, who is weary of repeating it, has a guarded look in his eyes. After botching the name a fourth time, I acknowledge defeat and attempt to apologize for my flawed linguistic performance. "I'm sorry, Charles, I can't get it. I'll work on it later, it's in the machine. It doesn't matter."

"It's matter," Charles says softly to me in English. And then, turning to speak to Morley, he addresses him in Western Apache:

> What he's doing isn't right. It's not good. He seems to be in a hurry. Why is he in a hurry? It's disrespectful. Our ancestors made this name. They made it just as it is. They made it for a reason. *They spoke it first, a long time ago!* He's repeating the speech of our ancestors. He doesn't know that. Tell him he's repeating the speech of our ancestors!

Charles's admonition, which Morley proceeds to translate without dulling its critical edge, leaves me unsettled and silent. That Charles has taken me for someone in a hurry comes as a surprise. Neither had I foreseen that my failure to pronounce the stubborn Apache placename would be interpreted by him as displaying a lack of respect. And never had I suspected that using Apache place-names might be heard by those who use them as repeating verbatim—actually quoting—the speech of their early ancestors. This is a fair amount to take in at once, and as the quiet of the morning asserts itself again, I fear that my actions, which were wholly unwitting but patently offensive, may have placed in jeopardy the future of our project. Charles and

Morley, put off by my incompetence, may now decide they have better things to do. Dammit!

But then, unexpectedly, in one of those courteous turnabouts that Apache people employ to assuage embarrassment and salvage damaged feelings, Charles himself comes to the rescue. With a quick corroborative grin, he announces he is missing several teeth and that my problem with the place-name may be attributable to his lack of dental equipment. Sometimes, he says, he is hard to understand—his nephew Jason recently told him that and he knows he tends to speak softly. Maybe the combination of too few teeth and too little volume accounts for my falling short. Morley, on the other hand, is not so encumbered. Though shy a tooth or two, he retains the good ones for talking, and because he is not afraid to speak up—except, as everyone knows, in the presence of garrulous women—no one has trouble hearing what he says. Maybe if Morley repeated the place-name again, slowly and with ample force, I would get it right. It's worth a try. Cousin?

"GOSHTŁ'ISH TÚ BIŁ SIKÁNÉ!" Rising to the spirit of Charles's playful teasing, Morley booms out the place-name, word by constituent word, with such exuberance as to startle into flight a pair of resident robins. All of us laugh as the birds wheel away, but for me the tide has turned. Instantly, the form of the name and its meaning assume coherent shape, and I know that at last I've got it: Goshtł'ish Tú Bił Sikáné, or Water Lies With Mud In An Open Container. Relieved and pleased, I pronounce the name slowly, then a bit more rapidly, and again as it might be spoken in normal conversation.[5] Charles listens and nods his head in approval. "Yes," he says in Apache. "That is how our ancestors made it a long time ago, just as it is to name this place." And then, keeping to his own language and speaking at times like an observer on the scene, he fashions a place-world in which the making and naming occurred.

They came to this country long ago, our ancestors did.
They hadn't seen it before, they knew nothing about it.
Everything was unfamiliar to them.
They were very poor. They had few possessions and
surviving was difficult for them. They were looking for a
good place to settle, a safe place without enemies. They were

searching. They were traveling all over, stopping here and there, noticing everything, looking at the land. They knew nothing about it and didn't know what they would find.

None of these places had names then, none of them did, and as the people went about they thought about this. "How shall we speak about this land?" they said. "How shall we speak about where we have been and where we want to go?"

Now they are coming! They are walking upstream from down below. Now they are arriving here, looking all about them, noticing everything about this place. It looked to them then as it looks to us now. We know that from its name—its name gives a picture of it, just as it was a long time ago.

Now they are happy. "This looks like a good place," they are saying to each other. Now they are noticing the plants that live around here. "Some of these plants are unknown to us. Maybe they are good for something. Maybe they are useful as medicines." Now they are saying, "This is a good place for hunting. Deer and turkey come here to eat and drink. We can wait for them here, hidden close by." They are saying that. They are noticing everything and talking about it together. They like what they see about this place. They are excited!

Now their leader is thinking, "This place may help us survive. If we settle in this country, we must be able to speak about this place and remember it clearly and well. We must give it a name."

So they named it Goshtł'ish Tú Bił Sikąné [Water Lies With Mud In An Open Container]. They made a picture of it with words. Now they could speak about it and remember it clearly and well. Now they had a picture they could carry in their minds. You can see for yourself. It looks like its name.

When Charles has finished speaking, he reaches down and takes from the marshy ground a heaping handful of mud. He squeezes it firmly, causing little jets of water to spurt from between his fingers. "There," he says with evident satisfaction. "Water and mud together, just as they were when our ancestors came here." He then excuses himself, explaining that he needs to procure a certain medicinal plant for use in his work at Cibecue; he will not be gone long and will join us back at the Jeep. Walking along with Morley, I cannot contain my appreciation for all that Charles has said. "That was great!" I exclaim. "It's like we were *there,* watching them when they came!" Morley concurs, adding matter of factly that Charles is a vigorous thinker and has done this sort of thing on numerous occasions. "Do you think he'll do it again?" I ask. "It's up to him," says Morley. "I think he probably will."

Snakes' Water

It turns out Morley is right. In the slow-moving week that follows (June is now upon us, the heat a relentless foe) we travel with Charles to twelve more places, and at two of these—an open expanse named Nadah Nch'íí' Golgaiyé (Bitter Agave Plain) and a dispersion of vertical boulders called Tséé Naadadn'áhá (Scattered Rocks Stand Erect)—he slips into the past and constructs ancestral place-worlds. Much as before, and speaking often in the same eyewitness voice, he imagines his forebears arriving on the scene, studying it intently, and assessing its potential for helping them survive. Looking out on Bitter Agave Plain, the ancestors marvel at all the grass, tall and thick and laden with edible seeds, and praise it as a sign of ample summer rainfall. Pausing at Scattered Rocks Stand Erect, they wonder with a mixture of fear and curiosity why the boulders are upright, as if rammed into the earth by some gigantic hand. At both localities they make and bestow a place-name, a name describing the place itself, just as it looked a long time ago, just as it looks today. And Charles, having lodged himself in the present again, says that much is contained in Apache place-names, preserving as they do both the words of his ancestors and their graphic impressions of an unfamiliar land.

But more is contained in Apache place-names than frozen ancestral quotes and ageless images of a new and striking landscape. In addition, place-names can offer evidence of changes in the landscape, showing clearly that certain localities do not present the appearance they did in former times. More interesting still, some of this evidence points to major shifts in local climatic patterns, thus allowing inferences to be drawn about how—and possibly why—the environment of the ancestors differed in key respects from that of their modern descendants. And were this not enough, the theme of places' changing even as they endure sometimes finds expression in gripping Apache place-worlds.

I knew nothing of these things until I accompanied Charles and Morley to Tłiish Bi Tú'é (Snakes' Water), an inactive spring at the foot of a sandstone bluff some miles west of Cibecue. Hidden from view by manzanita bushes, the spring is survived by a cluster of hand-cut rocks, flat and rectilinear, which encircle a pool of whitish sand, now the home of delicate purple wildflowers and a motley assortment of weeds. A Budweiser beer can, faded and pock-marked with rust, lies on the ground nearby. Standing alone a few feet away, Charles gazes at the rocks for several minutes, as though waiting for them to speak. And perhaps somehow they do, for he suddenly declares that the spring has long been dry, that at some point in time its water went away, and that the result of this is an absence of fit (a "lack of match" is what he says in Apache) between the place itself and the way its name describes it. The name it was given a long time ago shows that it has changed. Snake's Water, as anyone can see, is no longer the way it was when the ancestors saw it first and made it their own with words.

Motionless in denim shirt and sweat-stained Stetson hat, Charles again falls silent. Then, with his eyes still fixed on the barren circle of rocks, he begins to fashion a place-world in which they served an important purpose.

> Now these rocks are lying alone. No one comes to them anymore. Once this wasn't so. Long ago, people came here often. They squatted on these rocks when they filled their containers with water. They knelt on these rocks when they drank water from their hands. Our people were very grateful for this spring. It made them happy to know they could rely on it anytime. They were *glad* this place was here.
>
> Now they are coming to get water! They have been working—maybe they were digging up agave—and now they are thirsty. A man is walking in the lead with women and children behind him. The women are carrying their containers. Some have water jugs on their backs. No one is talking. Maybe there are snakes here, lying on these rocks. Yes! Now the man in front can see them! There are snakes lying stretched out on these rocks. They are the ones who own this spring, the ones who protect it.

Now that man is speaking to the people. "Listen to me," he is saying. "All of you must wait here. Don't go any closer. Don't approach Snakes' Water until I talk to them and ask them to move away." The people obey this man, knowing that he will do things correctly. Now they are waiting together in a group, just as he told them to do.

Now that man has come here. He is talking to those who protect Snakes' Water, using words they understand and doing things correctly. Soon they move off the rocks. They keep going, unalarmed, until they are out of sight. Now that man is sprinkling something on the water. It is a gift to the ones who own it. He is giving thanks to them and Water, informing them that he and the people are grateful. "This is good," he is saying to them. "This is good."

Now he is beckoning to the people to come and get water. Some of them are still concerned, holding back with their children. Others are arriving now, nervously looking around. Now they see they have nothing to fear—everything was done correctly—and they start to fill their containers. Now they are happy and grateful, talking amongst themselves. "This water is good," they are saying. "It is good that it is here for us." Some of the women are smiling. They know they have nothing to fear. Now they are kneeling on these stones, relieving their thirst, drinking from their hands.

Charles says no more—there is nothing to be said. The three of us turn from the barren spring and together walk slowly away, lost in thought and the deepness of time, sojourners still in a distant world that casts a powerful spell. A short while later, seated in the shade of a juniper tree, Charles explains that what we observed at Snakes' Water is not at all uncommon; there are more places like it, scattered throughout Apache country, that have undergone physical changes and no longer conform to the way their names describe them. Many of these places, he says, were named for sources of water—springs, seeps, bogs, seasonal pools at the bases of canyon walls—which now are permanently dry. Snakes' Water is a case in point, as are Dlǫ' Bi Tú'é (Birds' Water), another dry spring, and Tú Nłchǫ'é (Foul Water), a former seep, probably sulfurous, located far to the west. Other localities, according to their names, once gave life to species of plants that thrive under moist conditions, and these plants have either vanished or persist in stunted form. Tł'ohk'aa Sikaadé (Stand Of Arrow Cane), where today no cane exists, offers a telling example; so does T'iis Sikaadé (Grove Of Cottonwood Trees), where one small tree remains. And these are only a few.

Judging from what happened at these and other places, Charles goes on to say, there can be no doubt that the country was wetter and greener when the ancestors first explored it. This was one of the reasons, if not the major reason, they found it to their liking and decided to make it their home. For they were farmers as well as hunters—they had corn they wanted to plant—and they searched everywhere for water and its tell-tale signs. In this they were not disappointed, as their place–names plainly reveal. "The names do not lie," Charles states emphatically. "They show what is different and what is still the same." Like so many faithful photographs, he says, they record the look of the land as it was in ancestral times—and the look of the land was lush. It is less so today. Something must have happened. Water, obviously, began to go away.

After lighting a cigarette and pouring a cup of coffee from the thermos we carry with us, Charles volunteers that no one really knows (he implies with a shrug that no one really cares) when the water began to go away. It was sometime in the past, he says, and whether it happened slowly or fast, the people would have noticed and would have been concerned. There was water enough for life to go on—the streams still flowed and rains still came in the summer and fall—but it was definitely less abundant and its sources were less predictable. And this would have been interpreted as a punitive response, wrought by Water itself, to something the people had done. There *had* to be a reason for what was taking place, and the one most likely adduced, because it was the simplest and farthest-reaching, was that Water had been offended by acts of disrespect. Charles has wondered often what kinds of acts these were. Maybe, he says, the people were greedy, taking from springs and streams more water than they needed; maybe they were wasteful, throwing water away they should have been careful to save; or maybe they ceased doing everything correctly, neglecting in haste or forgetfulness to give repeated thanks to Water for giving of itself.

No one knows for sure, Charles says again, but no one doubts that the people were greatly alarmed to learn that they were at fault. He then travels back in his mind to the place from which we have come, imagining there the difficult day when a group of his ancestors, thirsty and eager to drink, discovered to their dismay that the spring at Snakes' Water was dry.

> The people came again to get water and saw that there was none. They were expecting it to be there. They were shocked! The women began to wail. The men stood silent and still. "Why has Snakes' Water dried up? Why has this happened? What have we done to cause this to happen? Water must surely be angry at us." This is what they are thinking.
>
> Now they are walking away, thirsty and shaking with fear. The women are wailing, louder and louder. Their children are crying, too. They are wailing as if a relative had died. "What if this happens elsewhere?! What if this happens everywhere?! What if Water takes all of itself away?!" They are deeply frightened because of what they have done.
>
> "Our holy people must work on this for us." This is what they are saying as they walk away from Snakes' Water. "Our holy people must help us by making amends to Water. They must help us so we may live! They must ask Water to take pity on us! What if this happened everywhere!" This is what they are thinking. This is what they are praying. They do not understand. They are terribly afraid. The women are wailing louder, as if a relative has died. Already they have started to pray.

Charles stands up and drinks the last of his coffee. The day is done. We return to the Jeep. On the drive back to Cibecue, no one says a word.

Juniper Tree Stands Alone

All ethnographers occasionally lose their snap, and so, of course, do those with whom they work. Rarely does the problem reach epic proportions, but it can happen. On a Saturday late in June, with nothing more in store than a quiet weekend in Cibecue, I was stung twice on the nose by hornets, broke my last pair of eyeglasses, and got bitten on the hand by an aggravated centipede while playing Aggravation, a locally popular board game, with three Apache enthusiasts; I also managed to run out of gas, which in Cibecue is taken as evidence of dangerously low intelligence. During the same eight-hour period, Morley received a very unfortunate haircut, tore his pants on a barbed-wire gate, and bought beer for a lady from out of town who responded to his kindness by trying to lift his wallet; he later sat down on a monstrous wad of bubblegum belonging to his six-year-old niece, who flew into a rage and attacked him with a dustpan. For his part, Charles woke up with a nasty stomach flu, sliced his hand on a can of Spam, and failed to amuse his wife when he wrapped the wound in one of her favorite dish towels; he later misplaced his pocketknife, a fairly worrisome loss, only to discover it in the pocket of his jacket. Taken all together, as more and more people rushed to observe, it was little short of hilarious, and when evening finally came, with Morley nursing a tender ego and me a bulbous nose, we went to call on Charles to see how he was doing.

Charles seemed happy to see us, proclaiming as we entered his house that everyone has uneven days, one might as well expect them, and that next to pails of Crisco and double-bladed axes—his wife, he supposes, would strongly favor dish towels—the whiteman's best invention may be Pepto-Bismol. He chuckles at the thought. Ensconced on a couch with his nephew Jason, he inquires whether I am pleased with the work we have done so far. When I tell him I am, he replies that more lies ahead because places and their names are important to Apache people in many different ways. Jason here, who just turned eleven, is learning this already, and once we resume our trips into the country—Jason, by the way, will be joining us when we do—he and I can learn together; soon, perhaps, we will take up the matter of Apache social lines, those close-knit groups of kin known to outsiders as "clans," whose names for themselves are really the names of places. Charles then changes the subject by beaming a smile at Morley. "I know my wife can't hear me," he says loudly in Apache, knowing that Mrs. Henry, who is close by in the kitchen, will pick up every word. "Speak to me, cousin, and don't leave anything out. What's this I hear about a beautiful widow from Whiteriver who made you tear your pants?"

Three days later, with Jason Henry in tow and the rest of us feeling revived, we are back upon the land. Rain has fallen the night before, steady and hard for more than an hour, and the colors of the country-side, no longer dull beneath layers of dust, look clean and freshly re-stored. The air smells sharp and fragrant. It is cool for the first time in weeks. The sky is a robust blue. On the northern outskirts of Cibecue we stop near a place named Gad 'O'ááhá (Juniper Tree Stands Alone), a large flat encompassing four Apache homes, two horse corrals, and at least a dozen acres planted in corn and beans. With coffee cup in hand, Charles surveys the scene, which could hardly be more peaceful. The morning light is soft and full, and the tilled red earth, darkened by the rain to a deep maroon, provides a striking backdrop to the bright green rows of maize. A dog barks. A door slams. A young sorrel mare rolls in some mud to keep away the flies. The land is fairly glowing in calm and radiant gratitude for the blessings brought by rain.

I cannot see a juniper tree, standing alone or otherwise, anywhere on the flat of Juniper Tree Stands Alone, a small but notable absence which prompts me to think that Charles may speak again about how the country has changed since his ancestors took it over. He does not. Reaching out his hand to the fields of growing corn, he performs a scooping motion that seems to gather them up, drawing them together as though cradled in his palm and setting the stage for a place-world about farm-ing and the origin of clans.

> They had wandered all over this country, looking at everything, searching for good places to live. They searched for places that would protect them from enemy people—the Navajo were one—so they made their homes high on the sides of valleys, nestled among the rocks. They also searched for places where they could plant their corn. They looked for these near streams or where there was runoff from rain.
>
> By now they knew the country well. They had given names to many places—like this one, Juniper Tree Stands Alone—and they thought they would survive and raise their families here. This country is where they would live and raise their children.

Now they are settling at different places. Some of them settled here—not right here on the flat, it would have exposed them to enemy people—but fairly close by, somewhere higher up, somewhere well concealed. This was long ago.

Now they are planting their corn here, not far from the stream, here on the flat. "Corn grows plentifully here," they are saying. "We have enough to eat and also to store away." They are grateful to Corn and to this place for helping them survive. They prayed often. Their prayers were strong. They did everything correctly. They were happy and grew confident.

They didn't stay here all the time. Some would make journeys to hunt for deer. Some would make journeys to dig and roast agave. Some would go off to collect seeds and cactus fruits. Some would go off for salt. But they would always return here in plenty of time to harvest their corn. They would roast and dry it. They saved its seeds to plant again. They kept dried corn to eat in winter and early spring, when they knew they would be hungry.

Now, long ago, those people who planted corn at Juniper Tree Stands Alone are coming back to harvest it. They have been off looking for acorns but have gathered only a few. Two or three older people have been left behind to watch over the corn. They are coming nearer now, the ones who have been away, praying and singing as they approach. They are praying that nothing has happened to injure or harm their corn. "What will we do if there is no corn?" they are thinking—but they are reluctant to say this out loud.

Now they can see their cornfields. There is much corn! There is corn in abundance! They are excited and happy. They know they will not go hungry. They know their prayers have been strong. "Juniper Tree Stands Alone has looked after us again."

Later, after getting their homes in order again, their leaders are talking. "This is where our women first planted corn. They have planted it again and again. Each year we have harvested enough to roast and dry and store away. These fields look after us by helping our corn to grow. Our children eat it and become strong. We eat it and continue to live. Our corn draws life from this earth and we draw life from our corn. This earth is part of us! We are *of* this place, Juniper Tree Stands Alone. We should name ourselves for this place. We are Gad 'O'ááhń [Juniper Tree Stands Alone People]. This is how it shall be.

Now the people spoke among themselves and agreed with what their leaders had said. They agreed to be known for the place where they first planted corn. Now they spoke of themselves to other people that way. "We are Juniper Tree Stands Alone People," they would say to them.

This would happen elsewhere, at many different places throughout the country. Groups of people named themselves for the places where their women first planted corn. That is why our lines [clans] go through women. That is why we belong to the line of our mother. We are *of* our mother's line and *for* the line of our father. It has always been that way.

You see, their names for themselves are really the names of their places. That is how they were known, to others and to themselves. They were known by their places. That is how they are still known, even though they have scattered and live now in many different states, some in cities far from here.

Many of the old cornfields are no longer planted. The people have forgotten about them. They say it's too much work to plant them as before. But some, like those Juniper Tree Stands Alone People, have not forgotten. They still plant their corn in the same place, as they have always done. Their corn still makes their children strong. This place still looks after them. It shows them where their ancestors returned, year after year, to harvest their corn and store it away for the winter.

As Charles is speaking, a woman who lives at Juniper Tree Stands Alone walks from her house to the edge of one of the cornfields, carrying over her arm an empty burlap sack and a folded canvas ground cloth. She is wearing a capacious blouse and a flowing, full-length skirt, both a shade of brilliant pink, and her loosely braided hair is generously streaked with gray. Her name is Ellen Josay Tessay. She is the leader of her clan, the oldest member and primary spokesperson of the Juniper Tree Stands Alone People. Charles watches in silence as she enters the cornfield, seats herself on her ground cloth, and begins to pull up weeds, placing them one by one inside the burlap sack. He then resumes his account, treating what he sees as a model of the past and transforming the figure of Ellen Tessay, carefully tending her corn, into a fully present symbol of what happened long ago.

The women looked after their corn, they looked after it well. The older people who stayed behind did this. They would go to their fields in the morning and stay there most of the day.

Now they are clearing the fields of unwanted plants, putting them in something to later take them away. "I am looking after you, just as I would my children," they are saying. "Because of this you will grow strong and tall and give us much to eat. I am praying this will happen."

They were careful to do everything correctly. They didn't rush or try to hurry their work. They depended on their corn, so they treated it with respect. This would help it to grow. They did everything correctly.

When Charles is done, Morley remarks that he owes two dollars to Ellen Tessay's husband, which he might as well give to her now. We follow Morley along a path to the cornfield where she is working. She greets our approach with a genial smile, inquiring of no one in particular, "What brings you here?" Morley explains the reason for our presence and goes on to settle his debt. He then delivers a compliment on the vigor of her corn. "It seems to be growing well," she modestly replies. "Last night's rain will help it even more." Moments later, she addresses Jason Henry, who is standing half-hidden behind his grandfather. "Young one, do you know what I am doing?" Caught off-guard by the directness of her question, Jason stares hard at the ground. "You are helping your corn," he responds in a faltering voice. Ellen Josay Tessay smiles again. "Yes," she says gently. "I'm looking after my children."

Shades Of Shit

It is now mid-July and our topographic maps of the Cibecue region are getting increasingly crowded. Dozens of dots and shaded areas mark the locations of places bearing Apache names, and numbers next to these index the names themselves, which are listed in separate notebooks. Morley says admiringly that some of the maps look like they were blasted with a shotgun—and more than once! Charles, modulated as always, expresses his approval in less effusive ways. Jason, who studies the maps whenever he gets a chance, has yet to voice an opinion. I am struck by the mounting number of named localities—we have charted 109 in only five weeks—and the consistent manner in which they cluster, mainly around sources of water and past and present farmsites.

But what impresses me most of all is the rich descriptive imagery of Western Apache place-names. Lately, with ear and eye jointly enthralled, I have stood before

Tséé Dotł'izh Ténaahijaahá (Green Rocks Side By Side Jut Down
Into Water; a group of mossy boulders on the bank of a stream)

Tséé Ditł'ige Naaditiné (Trail Extends Across Scorched Rocks;
a crossing at the bottom of a canyon)

T'iis Ts'ósé Bił Naagolgaiyé (Circular Clearing With Slender
Cottonwood Trees; a meadow)

Túzhį' Yaahigaiyé (Whiteness Spreads Out Descending To
Water; a sandstone cliff next to a spring)

Tséé Yaaditł'ishé (Line Of Blue Below Rocks; a mineral deposit)

Yaahiłbigé (Stunted Rising Up; a small mountain)

Kaiłbáyé Bił Naagozwodé (Gray Willows Curve Around
A Bend; a point on a stream)

and a number of other places whose handsomely crafted names—bold, visual, evocative—lend poetic force to the voices of the ancestors.

Just as expressive are other Apache place-names, different from these, that do not give close descriptions of the places to which they refer. Commemorative in character and linked to traditional stories, they allude instead to historical events that illuminate the causes and consequences of wrongful social conduct. And in this important capacity, as I would discover at a place named Shades Of Shit (Chąą Bi Dałt'ohé), they invest the Apache landscape with a sobering moral dimension, dark but instructive, that place-makers can exploit to deeply telling effect.

The shades, or brush-covered ramadas, are no longer standing. They collapsed, Charles says, a long time ago. Yet the place where they stood, a tree-covered knoll southwest of Cibecue, is avoided to this day. "No one wants to come here," he explains, as we slowly approach a vantage point a hundred yards away. "The people who lived here had farms down below, probably next to the creek. This was long after they settled in this valley. Then they did something bad, very bad, and they came close to dying. There is a story about it I was told by my grandfather. It's short." And it is . . .

> It happened here at Shades Of Shit.
> They had much corn, those people who lived here,
> and their relatives had only a little. They refused to share it.
> Their relatives begged them but still they refused to share it.
>
> Then their relatives got angry and forced them to stay at home. They wouldn't let them go anywhere, not even to defecate. So they had to do it at home. Their shades filled up with it. There was more and more of it! It was very bad! Those people got sick and nearly died.
>
> Then their relatives said, "You have brought this on yourselves. Now you live in shades of shit!" Finally, they agreed to share their corn.
>
> It happened at Shades Of Shit.

An uneasy silence settles over our group. Jason looks suddenly wan. Morley spits in disgust. A soft breeze, recalling a terrible stench it could not possibly carry, ruffles the morning air. When Charles speaks again, he says that he wonders what really happened here: it couldn't have been as simple as the story suggests. And even if it were, he adds, the story gives no sense of why events unfolded as they did or how the people involved might have reacted to them. "What were they *think-*

ing?" he asks rhetorically in a tone of disbelief. "How must they have *felt?*" Charles would like to know these things, he says, though he doubts he ever will. And then, speaking as if he knew them very well, he tells his grandfather's story again, fleshing it out at length and constructing for us an astonishing world as surely revealing of Apache social values as it is violently offensive to their most basic sensibilities.

It must have been late in the summer. Those people had harvested their corn and were drying it and roasting it. They must have been grateful and happy. "Now we have much to eat," they are saying.

Their relatives envied them. Their own corn had not grown well. (Sometimes it happens that way. Some fields produce a lot, and those right next to them do not. It happens that way, and no one knows why, and sometimes they talk of witchcraft prompted by revenge for something that was done to them in the past.) Their own corn was meager and small but they were not yet afraid or angry. "Our more fortunate relatives will help us," they said, speaking among themselves. "They have more than enough corn. They will want to share it with us. We have always helped each other. That is how it should be."

Then they waited for their relatives to help them. They waited in vain. Their relatives kept their corn to themselves, eating it every day and making big shits when they went off into the brush. They did nothing for their relatives, although they noticed their plight. "They have enough food, even though they harvested little corn. They probably have plenty of beans and squash. Some of them are skilled hunters. Soon they will have plenty of deer meat to eat. We will keep our corn for ourselves, so that our children will not be hungry during the winter."

Now their poor relatives are becoming scared and puzzled. "Why do they not offer to help us?" they said. "They're treating us like we don't exist, as if we are nothing to them. We will have a hard time unless they change their minds and give us some of their corn."

Then they sent someone to talk to the people who lived here. "We are your relatives," he said to them. "We must help each other. You have plenty of corn. We have seen it. But we have only a little and soon it will be gone. Soon our children will be crying because they have nothing to eat. Give us some of your corn. Give us some of your corn. We will be grateful. This is how it should be."

Then they waited again, and still their relatives did nothing for them. They talked again among themselves. "Our relatives are not going to help us," they said. "They have become greedy and stingy. They think only of themselves. They have put themselves above us, ignoring us like we don't exist. We have waited long enough. We must do something!"

Then they became angry at their own relatives. "We will make them stay at their homes. They will not go anywhere. We will make them live with their own big shits!" This is what they decided to do.

Then they came over here and surrounded their relatives' homes. They told them to stay there. They did this day and night. "We will harm you if you try to leave," they said. "You have brought this on yourselves. You can eat all you want. Only now you will shit at your homes. This is not how it should be, but we are doing it anyway," they said.

Then those people must have thought they were joking. "They don't really mean what they say," they said. "They will not harm us," they said. So they chose a man to leave his home. He was forced back by his relatives. Another man tried to leave. He was also forced back. "They mean what they say," they said. "Now we are in for trouble," they thought.

Then they started to shit in their shades. Some of them said, "This is very bad. We should share our corn and put an end to it." Others said, "No! If we give away some of our corn, they will want it all. We must not give in to them. This is their way of leaving us with nothing."

Then they ate less and less but still they fouled their shades. There was more and more of it! It was visible everywhere! The sight and smell could not be avoided! There were swarms and swarms of flies! Huge swarms! They no longer cooked in their shades. Eating became something they detested. It was terrible!

Then they started to get sick from the sight and smell of their own filth. Some of them were constantly dizzy. Others had trouble walking straight. Their children started moaning. They themselves were moaning. "We could die from this!" they said. "We could die from our own filth."

Then a man of the people who had little corn went and talked to them. "You have brought this on yourselves," he said. "You should have shared your corn with us as soon as you knew you had more than enough. You didn't do this! You gave us nothing at all. You were greedy and stingy, thinking only of yourselves. Because of this we had to beg you to share your corn with us. Even then, you did nothing. You just kept on eating, more and more, knowing that we had little food of our own. You ignored us—your own relatives—as if we were nothing! This is not how it should be. As relatives we make each other rich because we help each other in times of need. It has been this way since the beginning. What made you forget this? What made you ignore us? Well, I don't know. But now you live in shades of shit! Now you are getting sick!"

Then he laughed at them. He laughed at them.

Then those people talked among themselves. "What he says is true," they said. "*Look what has become of us!* We were thinking only of ourselves. Our greed is responsible for our trouble. We looked down on our own relatives and gave them nothing. Look what has become of us!"

Then they shared their corn. Finally, they did this. Their relatives took the corn away, saying nothing, saying nothing. Now those people were allowed to leave their homes.

Then those people said, "We must leave here and go somewhere else to live. This is a bad place. It stinks with signs of our stinginess and greed."

"It could have happened that way," Charles says almost casually. And then, a bit sternly, "Let's move on. We've been here long enough."

During the next two weeks, we visit other places with Apache commemorative names, and Charles relates the stories that explain their origins and supply their cultural backing. At several of these places, as at Shades of Shit, he finds the stories threadbare and proceeds to enlarge upon them, building historical place-worlds with ease and consummate skill. Each story is concerned with disruptive social acts, with everyday life gone out of control, and each concludes with a stark reminder that trouble would not have occurred if people had behaved in ways they knew they should. Each depicts the anguish of those who erred and the depth of their regret. For me, riveted and moved, the country takes on a different cast, a density of meaning—and with it a formidable strength—it did not have before. Here, there, and over there, I see, are places which proclaim by their presence and their names both the imminence of chaos and the preventive wisdom of moral norms. "Don't make mistakes," these places seem to say. "Think sensibly and do what is right. For therein goodness lies, the goodness inherent in established patterns of social order, and therein lies survival."

These are my thoughts at Widows Pause For Breath ('Istaa Hadaanáyołé), a grassy flat with sunflowers, where three Apache sisters keened for several days after learning that their husbands, with whom they had violated sexual proscriptions, had died in a raid against some Navajos. And again at They Piled On Top Of Each Other ('Iłk'eejijeedé), a former gambling ground where a man was killed and others injured in a furious brawl triggered by unfounded accusations of cheating during a high-stakes match for horses. And again at Navajos Are Coming! (Yúdahą́ Kaikaiyé), a winding draw where four Apache families avoided certain ambush when an alert young woman heard a horse whose nicker she did not recognize; a complacent sentry, supposedly on guard, was asleep at his post, having drunk too much *tułibai* (literally, 'gray water'), a native beverage made from corn.

The commemorative place–names, accompanied by their stories, continue to accumulate, each one marking the site of some sad or tragic event from which valuable lessons can be readily drawn and taken fast to heart. And these names too, like their more descriptive counterparts, have a poetry of their own, a song they sing, haunting and provocative, in a voice as old as Apaches on the land. Place-names such as

Sáan Łeezhiteezhé (Two Old Women Are Buried; a hill)

Tú 'Ahiyi'ee Nzįné (They Are Grateful For Water; a small flat close to an arroyo)

Na'ishǫ́ Bitsit'iiyé (Lizards Dart Away In Front; the eastern face of a mountain)

Kolah Dahch'ewoołé (She Carries Her Brother On Her Back; a steep slope)

Są́ Silį́į Sidáhá (She Became Old Sitting; a cornfield)

Ták'eh Godzigé (Rotten Field; another cornfield)

'Ihi'na' Ha'itin (Trail To Life Goes Up; a butte)

Chagháshé Biké'é (Children's Footprints; a rock in an evanescent stream)

Dǫ́' Bigowąné (Fly's Camp; an ephemeral spring)

and many more besides.

On the second day of August, while drinking coffee near a sandstone formation named Tséé Łitsog Deez'áhá (Yellow Rocks Jut Out), Charles announces that he will work with us no more. There are plants he needs to collect, medicines he must make, and he is counting on Jason to help him until the start of school. He also notes that Morley and I have yet to translate some of the tapes he made during the summer, and this, of course, will take time; it would not be wise for us (he means me) to do it in a hurry. Charles seems relieved with his decision to leave our project, glad that his time will again be his own to do with as he chooses. Autumn is not far off—the clouds have told him that—and now is none too soon to begin to prepare for winter. He is obviously eager to get on with other things.

But Charles is not finished teaching. Fingering his hat and looking at the ground, he recalls the day in May when he explained to me that Western Apache place-names were created by his ancestors, that they were—and are—his ancestors' very own words. Now, he believes, I know this to be so. He also wants me to know that our travels together were planned by him to reflect the changing conditions under which the names were conferred. Descriptive place-names came first, he reminds me, bestowed at a time when his ancestors were exploring the land and deciding to make it their home. The names of clans, which are based upon descriptive place-names, came later, when the land was being settled and people had gathered in the vicinity of farms. Commemorative names were awarded last, after the Apaches had made the land their own and were experiencing the rewards—and also the painful problems—that come with community living. (Additional names, he goes on to say, have been coined in recent times, in English as well as in Apache, but these are fairly few and of relatively minor consequence.) The point Charles wishes to make is one he made before—that whenever one uses a place-name, even unthinkingly, one is quoting ancestral speech—and that is not only good but something to take seriously. It is something, he says, to think about.

And now it is time to go. Morley looks downcast and I am feeling sad. We will miss our days in the country with Charles. Stumbling over my words, I try to thank him for all he has done. He listens, nods, and once again takes steps to relieve an awkward moment. "Jason needs to drink pop," he says brightly. "Maybe Orange Crush. Morley, you need a Reese Cup!" And then, adjusting his well-worn hat, Charles Henry smiles and turns to walk back to the Jeep.

Place-worlds and Western Apache History

In 1962, the distinguished anthropologist Edward N. Spicer observed somewhat wistfully that Western Apache people, while plainly interested in their own tribal history, showed very little interest in becoming tribal historians.

> Curiously enough, the Western Apache are one of the most written about peoples of the Southwest and yet they remain, in my opinion, the most poorly understood by whitemen. Apaches complain constantly that all the history in print misrepresents them, yet so far no Apache autobiographer or even a rough chronicler has emerged. Perhaps we may expect that development within the next few years. (Spicer 1962:593)

Today, more than thirty years later, one could still maintain that the Western Apaches have yet to produce a tribal historian—but only were one to judge, as Spicer did, by Anglo-American standards of what historians are and how they practice their craft. And there, of course, is the rub. For by now it should be clear that Apache standards for interpreting the past are not the same as our own, and that working Apache historians—Charles Henry among them—go about their business with different aims and procedures. It may also have been surmised that few Apache people would wish to change these procedures, much less abandon them, and that Spicer's call to adopt another approach will probably go unheeded for quite some time to come. But why? Why the resistance? What is it about established Apache practices for exploring tribal history that Apache men and women find so attractive and rewarding? And why are certain Anglo-American practices, such as crafting extended chronicles and presenting autobiographies, tangential to their interests and unsuited to their tastes? What, in short, creates the evident gulf between these two conflicting perspectives on making useful visits to the country of the past?

As conceived by Apaches from Cibecue, the past is a well-worn 'path' or 'trail' (*'intin*) which was traveled first by the people's founding ancestors and which subsequent generations of Apaches have traveled ever since. Beyond the memories of living persons, this path is no longer visible—the past has disappeared—and thus it is unavailable for direct consultation and study. For this reason, the past must be constructed—which is to say, imagined—with the aid of historical materials, sometimes called 'footprints' or 'tracks' (*biké' goz'ą́ą́*), that have survived into the present.[6] These materials come in various forms, including Apache place-names, Apache stories and songs, and different kinds of relics found at locations throughout Apache country (the hand-cut stones surrounding the spring at Snakes' Water provide a good example). Because no one knows when these phenomena came into being, locating past events in time can be accomplished only in a vague and general way. This is of little consequence, however, for what matters most to Apaches is *where* events occurred, not when, and what they serve to reveal about the development and character of Apache social life. In light of these priorities, temporal considerations, though certainly not irrelevant, are accorded secondary importance.

For people like Charles Henry and Morley Cromwell, the country of the past—and with it Apache history—is never more than a narrated place-world away. It is thus very near, as near as the workings of their own imaginations, and can be easily brought to life at almost any time. It is history constructed in spurts, in sudden bursts of imaginative activity, and it takes the form of stories delivered in spoken Apache, the language of the ancestors and most of their modern descendants. Answering the question "What happened here?", it deals in the main with single events, and because these are tied to places within Apache territory, it is pointedly local and unfailingly episodic. It is also extremely personal, consistently subjective, and therefore highly variable among those who work to produce it. For these and other reasons, it is history without authorities—all narrated place-worlds, provided they seem plausible, are considered equally valid—and the idea of compiling "definitive accounts" is rejected out of hand as unfeasible and undesirable. Weakly empirical, thinly chronological, and rarely written down, Western Apache history as practiced by Apaches advances no theories, tests no hypotheses, and offers no general models. What it does instead, and likely has done for centuries, is fashion possible worlds, give them expressive shape, and present them for contemplation as images of the past that can deepen and enlarge awareness of the present. In the country of the past, as Apaches like to explore it, the place-maker is an indispensable guide.

And this in a powerful sense. For the place-maker's main objective is to speak the past into being, to summon it with words and give it dramatic form, to *produce* experience by forging ancestral worlds in which others can participate and readily lose themselves. To this engrossing end, as Charles Henry showed repeatedly, the place-maker often speaks as a witness on the scene, describing ancestral events "as they are occurring" and creating in the process a vivid sense that what happened long ago—right here, on this very spot—could be happening *now*. Within this narrative frame, all is movement and animated talk: the ancestors come and go, voicing their thoughts and feelings, always engaged in pressing activities (naming places and clans, cultivating corn, guarding against enemies), occasionally elated, often subdued, constantly concerned with staying alive. Leaders lead, followers follow, and most of the time things are done correctly. But now and again mistakes are made, serious trouble ensues, and social life is shattered. Pathos reigns and the air is charged with suspense. What will happen next? What will the ancestors do? How will they survive?

Thus performed and dramatized, Western Apache place-making becomes a form of narrative art, a type of historical theater in which the "pastness" of the past is summarily stripped away and long-elapsed events are made to unfold as if before one's eyes. It is history given largely in the active present tense ("Now they are arriving. . ."), and it makes extensive use of quoted speech to enter the hearts and minds of those whom it portrays ("Our relatives will not harm us," they said; "Now we are in for trouble," they thought). It is typically concise, tends to be closely plotted, and rarely becomes redundant. It thrives on verisimilitude ("There were swarms and swarms of flies. Huge swarms!"), and what it may lack in subtlety is more than offset by moments of intense urgency and involvement with its subjects (*"Look what has become of us now!"*). Its principal themes are the endless quest for survival, the crucial importance of community and kin, and the beneficial consequences, practical and otherwise, of adhering to moral norms. Accordingly, one of its basic aims is to instill empathy and admiration for the ancestors themselves—they came, they settled, they toiled, they endured—and to hold them up to all as worthy of emulation, except, of course, when they fail to do what is right and threaten by their actions the welfare of the group; then they are punished or killed.

By comparison, Western Apache history of the Anglo-American variety strikes many Apache people as distant and unfamiliar.[7] Unspoken and unanimated, it lies silent and inert on the printed English page; it is history without voices to thrust it into the present. Removed from the contexts of daily social life (reading, Apaches have noticed, is an isolating activity), it also seems unconnected to daily affairs and concerns; it is history without discernible applications. Detached from the local Apache landscape, it has few spatial anchors, and when places are identified, as often they are not, their names are not their own; it is history loosely situated, geographically adrift. Obsessed with dating historical events, it packs them into tightly ordered sequences which it then may try to explain by invoking abstract forces ("mounting tribal aggression" and

"outbreaks of cultural disarray" were two of Morley Cromwell's fa-
vorites) in which no one can quite believe; it thus becomes remote,
intangible, divorced in suspect ways from the forces of human agency.
Commonly qualified and sometimes hotly debated by persons who construct it, it appears to be in search of final historical truths, of which
Apaches believe there are very few indeed; it can therefore seem arrogant and misguided, pretending to large discoveries it could not possibly
make. And it does go on and on, persistently uninformed by the views
of Apache people, suggesting quite improbably that useful accounts of
history can and should be fashioned without consulting those whose
history it is. Add to this that it has almost nothing to say about the
people's early ancestors, and that recognizable place-worlds are virtually
nonexistent, and you have a set of practices which by Western Apache
standards rather miss the mark. Apache tribal history as crafted by Anglo-
Americans proceeds on different assumptions, produces a different discourse, and involves a different aesthetic.[8] Mute and unperformed,
sprawling in its way over time and space alike, it strikes Apache audi-
ences as dense, turgid, and lacking in utility. But far more important is
the fact that it does not excite. It does not captivate. It does not *engage*
and provoke a measure of wonder. As Charles Henry said once in English, summing up quite a bit, "It's pretty mainly quiet. It stays far away
from all our many places."[9]

Staying away from places is something that Western Apaches would
not recommend, and in this pervasive conviction they are not alone. As
Vine Deloria, Jr. (Standing Rock Sioux), has observed, most American
Indian tribes embrace "spatial conceptions of history" in which places
and their names—and all that these may symbolize—are accorded central importance.[10] For Indian men and women, the past lies embedded
in features of the earth—in canyons and lakes, mountains and arroyos,
rocks and vacant fields—which together endow their lands with multiple forms of significance that reach into their lives and shape the ways
they think. Knowledge of places is therefore closely linked to knowledge of the self, to grasping one's position in the larger scheme of things,
including one's own community, and to securing a confident sense of
who one is as a person. With characteristic eloquence, N. Scott Momaday
(Kiowa) suggests that this has been so for a very long time.

From the time the Indian first set foot upon this continent, he centered his life in the natural world. He is deeply invested in the earth, committed to it both in his consciousness and in his instinct. The sense of place is paramount. Only in reference to the earth can he persist in his identity. (Momaday 1994:1)

In the Western Apache case, this is certainly true. The people's sense of place, their sense of their tribal past, and their vibrant sense of themselves are inseparably intertwined. Their identity has persisted. Their ancestors saw to this, and in the country of the past, where the ancestors come alive in resonating place-worlds, they do so still today. Their voices are strong and firm—and sometimes it is unclear who is quoting whom.[11]

Stalking with Stories

*American Indians hold their lands—places—as having the highest possible meaning,
and all their statements are made with this reference point in mind.*
—*Vine Deloria, Jr.*, God Is Red

Shortly before his death in 1960, Clyde Kluckhohn made the following observation in a course he gave at Harvard University on the history of anthropological thought: "The most interesting claims people
make are those they make about themselves. Cultural anthropologists
should keep this in mind, especially when they are doing fieldwork."
Although Kluckhohn's comment seemed tenuously connected to the
topic of his lecture (he was speaking that day on the use of statistical
methods in culture-and-personality studies), few of his students were
distracted or annoyed. We had discovered early on that some of his
most provocative thoughts came in the form of brief asides delivered
casually and without apology at unexpected moments. We also learned
that these ostensibly offhand remarks frequently contained advice on
a topic that we were eager to know more about: ethnography and
ethnographic research. Rarely, however, did Kluckhohn see fit to elaborate on his advice, and so it was only later, after some of us had become
ethnographers ourselves, that we could begin to assess it properly.

I think that in this instance Kluckhohn was right. Attending carefully to claims that people make about themselves, and then trying to
grasp with some exactness what they have claimed and why, can be a
perplexing and time-consuming business. But when the work goes
well—when puzzling claims are seen to make principled sense and
when, as a consequence of this, one is able to move closer to an un-

37

derstanding of who the people involved take themselves to be—it can be richly informative and highly worthwhile. Indeed, as Kluckhohn implied in his textbook *Mirror for Man* (1949), it is just this sort of work that makes ethnography the singularly valuable activity—and, he might have added, the singularly arresting and gratifying one—it very often is.

This chapter focuses on a small set of spoken texts in which members of the community of Cibecue express claims about themselves, their language, and the lands on which they live. The statements that interest me, which could be supplemented by a large number of others, are the following.

> The land is always stalking people. The land makes people
> live right. The land looks after us. The land looks after people.
> (Annie Peaches, age 77, 1978)

> Our children are losing the land. It doesn't go to work on
> them anymore. They don't know the stories about what
> happened at these places. That's why some get into trouble.
> (Ronnie Lupe, age 42; Chairman, White Mountain Apache
> Tribe, 1978)

> We used to survive only off the land. Now it's no longer that
> way. Now we live only with money, so we need jobs. But the
> land still looks after us. We know the names of the places
> where everything happened. So we stay away from badness.
> (Nick Thompson, age 64, 1980)

> I think of that mountain called Tséé Łigai Dah Sidilé (White
> Rocks Lie Above In A Compact Cluster) as if it were my
> maternal grandmother. I recall stories of how it once was at
> that mountain. The stories told to me were like arrows.
> Elsewhere, hearing that mountain's name, I see it. Its name is
> like a picture. Stories go to work on you like arrows. Stories
> make you live right. Stories make you replace yourself.
> (Benson Lewis, age 64, 1979)

One time I went to L.A., training for mechanic. It was no
good, sure no good. I start drinking, hang around bars all the
time. I start getting into trouble with my wife, fight sometimes
with her. It was bad. I forget about this country here around
Cibecue. I forget all the names and stories. I don't hear them
in my mind anymore. I forget how to live right, forget how to
be strong. (Wilson Lavender, age 52, 1975)

If these statements resist easy interpretation, it is not because the
people who made them are confused or cloudy thinkers. Neither is it
because, as one unfortunate commentator would have us believe, the
Western Apache are "mystically inclined and correspondingly inar-
ticulate." The problem we face is a semiotic one, a barrier to constructing appropriate sense and significance which arises from the fact
that all views articulated by Apache people are informed by their experience in a culturally constituted world of objects and events with
which most of us are unfamiliar. What sort of world is it? Or, to draw
the question into somewhat sharper focus, what is the cultural context
in which Apache statements such as the foregoing find acceptance as
valid claims about reality?

More specifically still, what is required to interpret Annie Peaches's
claim that the land occupied by the Western Apache is "always stalking people" and that because of this they know how to "live right"?
How should we understand Chairman Lupe's assertion that Apache
children sometimes misbehave because the land "doesn't go to work
on them any more"? Why does Nick Thompson claim that his knowledge of place-names and historical events enables him to "stay away
from badness"? Why does Benson Lewis liken place-names to pictures,
stories to arrows, and a mountain near Cibecue to his maternal grandmother? And what should we make of Wilson Lavender's recollec-
tion of an unhappy time in California when forgetting place-names
and stories caused him to forget "how to be strong"? Are these claims
structured in metaphorical terms, or are they, given Western Apache
assumptions about the physical universe and the place of people within
it, somehow to be interpreted literally? In any case, what is the reasoning that lies behind the claims, the informal logic of which they are

simultaneously products and expressions? Above all, what makes the claims make sense?

I shall address these and other questions through an investigation of how Western Apaches talk about the natural landscape and the importance they attach to named locations within it. Accordingly, my discussion focuses on elements of language and patterns of speech, my purpose being to learn from these elements and patterns something of how Apache people construe their land and render it intelligible. Whenever Apaches describe the land—or, as happens more frequently, whenever they tell stories about incidents that have occurred at specific points upon it—they take steps to constitute it in relation to themselves. Which is simply to observe that in acts of speech, mundane and otherwise, Apaches fashion images and understandings of the land that are accepted as credible accounts of what it actually is, why it is significant, and how it impinges on the daily lives of men and women. In short, portions of a world view are constructed and made available, and a Western Apache version of the landscape is deepened, amplified, and tacitly affirmed. With words, a massive physical presence is fashioned into a meaningful human universe.

This universe of meanings comprises the cultural context in which the Western Apache texts presented earlier acquire their validity and appropriateness. Consequently, if we are to understand the claims set forth in these statements, portions of that context must be explored and made explicit. We must proceed, in other words, by relating our texts to other aspects of Western Apache thought—in effect, to other texts and other claims—and continue doing this, more and more comprehensively, until finally it is possible to confront the texts directly and expose the major premises on which they rest. As we shall see, most of these premises are grounded in an unformalized native model of Western Apache storytelling which holds that oral narratives have the power to establish enduring bonds between individuals and features of the natural landscape, and that as a direct consequence of such bonds, persons who have acted improperly will be moved to reflect critically on their misconduct and resolve to improve it. A native model of how stories work to shape Apaches' conceptions of the landscape, it is also a model of how stories work to shape Apaches' conceptions

of themselves. Ultimately, it is a model of how two symbolic resources—language and the land—are manipulated by Apaches to promote compliance with standards for acceptable social behavior and
the moral values that support them.

Should it appear, then, that these Western Apache texts lack either
substance or complexity, we shall see that in fact both qualities are
present in ample measure. And should the aim of interpreting such
modestly worded documents seem unduly narrow, or my strategy for
trying to accomplish it too tightly bound up with an examination of
linguistic and ethnographic particulars, it will become evident soon
enough that wider and more general issues are very much involved.
Of these, I shall suggest, none is more pressing or conspicuous than
the reluctance of cultural ecologists to deal openly and in close detail
with the symbolic attributes of human environments and the effects of
environmental constructions on patterns of social action.

But I am getting ahead of myself. The problem now is how to get
started, and for advice on that matter I turn here, as I actually did in
Cibecue a number of years ago, to a gifted and unusual man. Teacher
and consultant, serious thinker and salacious joker alike, he has so
strongly influenced the content and organization of this essay that he
has become, with his permission, a part of it himself—and so, too, of
the interpretation it presents.

"Learn the Names"

Nick Thompson is, by his own admission, an old man. It is possible, he told me once, that he was born in 1918. Beneath snow-white
hair cut short, his face is round and compact, his features small and
sharply molded. His large, black, and very bright eyes move quickly,
and when he smiles he acquires an expression that is at once mischie-
vous and intimidating. I have known him for more than twenty years,
and he has instructed me often on matters pertaining to Western Apache
language and culture. A man who delights in play, he has also teased
me unmercifully, concocted humorous stories about me that are thoroughly apocryphal, and embarrassed me before large numbers of in-
credulous Apaches by inquiring publicly into the most intimate details
of my private life. Described by many people in Cibecue as a true

Slim Coyote (Ma' Ts'ósé), Nick Thompson is outspoken, incorrigible, and unabashed.[1] He is also generous, thoughtful, and highly intelligent. I value his friendship immensely.

As I bring my Jeep to a halt on the road beside the old man's camp, I hear Nick complaining loudly to his wife about the changing character of life in Cibecue and its regrettable effects on younger members of the community. I have heard these complaints before and I know they are deeply felt. But still, on this sunny morning in June 1980, it is hard to suppress a smile, for the image Nick presents, a striking example of what can be achieved with sartorial bricolage, is hardly what one would expect of a staunch tribal conservative. Crippled since childhood and partially paralyzed by a recent stroke, the old man is seated in the shade of a cottonwood tree a few yards from the modest wooden cabin where he lives with his wife and two small grandchildren. He is smoking a Salem cigarette and studying with undisguised approval the shoes on his feet—a new pair of bright blue Nike running shoes trimmed in incandescent orange. He is also wearing a pair of faded green trousers, a battered brown cowboy hat, and a white T-shirt with "Disneyland" printed in bold red letters across the front. Within easy reach of his chair, resting on the base of an upended washtub, is a copy of the *National Enquirer,* a mug of hot coffee, and an open box of chocolate-covered doughnuts. If Nick Thompson is an opponent of social change, it is certainly not evident from his appearance. But appearances can be deceiving, and Nick, who is an accomplished singer and a medicine man of substantial reputation, would be the first to point this out.

The old man greets me with his eyes. Nothing is said for a minute or two, but then we begin to talk, exchanging bits of local news until enough time has passed for me to politely announce the purpose of my visit. I explain that I am puzzled by certain statements Apaches have made about the country surrounding Cibecue and I am eager to know how to interpret them. To my surprise, Nick does not ask what I have been told or by whom. He responds instead by swinging his arm out in a wide arc. "Learn the names," he says. "Learn the names of all these places." Unprepared for such a firm and unequivocal suggestion (it sounds to me like nothing less than an order), I retreat into silence. "Start with the names," the old man continues. "I will teach you like before. Come back tomorrow morning." Nodding in agreement, I thank Nick for his willingness to help and tell him what I will be able to pay him. He says the wage is fair.

A few minutes later, as I stand to take my leave, Nick's face breaks suddenly into a broad smile and his eyes begin to dance. I know that look well and brace myself for the farewell joke that almost always accompanies it. The old man wastes no time. He says I look lonely. He urges me to have prolonged and abundant sex with very old women. He says it prevents nosebleeds. He says that someday I can write a book about it. Flustered and at a loss for words, I smile weakly and shake my head. Delighted with this reaction, Nick laughs heartily and reaches for his coffee and a chocolate-covered doughnut.

I return to the old man's camp the following day and start to learn Western Apache place-names. My lessons, which are interrupted by mapping trips with more mobile Apache consultants, continue for the next ten weeks. In late August, shortly before I must leave Cibecue, Nick asks to see the maps. He is not impressed. "White men need paper maps," he observes. "We have maps in our minds."

Western Apache Place-names

The study of American Indian place-name systems has fallen on hard times. Once a viable component of anthropology in the United States, it has virtually ceased to exist, the inconspicuous victim of changing intellectual fashions and large amounts of ethnographic neglect. There are good reasons for advocating a revival. As early as 1900, Franz Boas, who was deeply impressed by the minutely detailed environmental knowledge of the Baffin Land and Hudson Bay Eskimos, suggested that one of the most profitable ways to explore the "mental life" of Indian peoples was to investigate their geographical nomenclatures (Boas 1901–1907). In 1912, Edward Sapir made the same point in more general terms, saying that Indian vocabularies provided valuable insight into native conceptions of the natural world and much that was held to be significant within it. Later, in 1934, Boas published a short monograph entitled *Geographical Names of the Kwakiutl Indians*. This essay is essentially a study of Kwakiutl word morphology, but it demonstrates beautifully Boas's earlier ideas concerning the Eskimos: that the study of place-name systems may reveal a great deal about the cognitive categories with which environmental phenomena are organized and understood. This tradition of research, which also included J. P. Harrington's (1916) massive treatise on Tewa place-names, began to falter in the years preceding World War II. A few brief articles appeared in the 1950s, and Floyd Lounsbury contributed an important paper on Iroquois place-names in 1960. Since then, however, little work has been done. Indeed, with the notable exception of Frederica de Laguna's (1972) long-delayed monograph on the Tlingit, I know of not a single study written by a linguist or anthropologist in the past twenty-five years that deals extensively or in depth with the place-name system of a North American tribe.[2]

One can only imagine how Boas or Sapir might have reacted to Nick Thompson's interest in Western Apache place-names. They would have been intrigued, I think, but probably not surprised. For each of them had come to understand, as I would at Cibecue, that American Indian place-names are intricate little creations and that studying their internal structure, together with the functions they serve in spoken conversation, can lead the ethnographer to any number of useful discoveries. All that is required is sound instruction from able native consultants, a fondness for mapping extensive areas of territory, and a modest capacity for wonder and delight at the large tasks that small words can be made to perform. And one more thing: a willingness to reject the widely accepted notion that place-names are nothing more than handy vehicles of reference. Place-names do refer, and quite indispensably at that, but in communities such as Cibecue, they are used and valued for other reasons as well.[3]

Located in a narrow valley at an elevation of 4,900 feet, the settlement at Cibecue (from Deeschii' Bikoh, Valley With Long Red Bluffs) is bisected by a shallow stream emanating from springs that rise in low-lying mountains to the north. Apache homes, separated by horse pastures, agricultural plots, and ceremonial dance grounds, are located on both sides of the stream for a distance of approximately ten miles. The valley itself, bounded on the east and west by a series of red sandstone bluffs, displays marked topographic diversity in the form of heavily dissected canyons and arroyos, broad alluvial floodplains, and several clusters of prominent peaks. Vegetation ranges from a mixed ponderosa pine-douglas fir association near the headwaters of Cibecue Creek to a chaparral community consisting of scrub oak, catclaw, agave, and a variety of cactus species at the confluence of the creek with the Salt River. In between, numerous other floral associations occur, including dense riparian communities and heavy stands of cottonwood, oak, walnut, and pine.

Together with Charles Henry, Morley Cromwell, and other Apache consultants, I have mapped nearly forty-five square miles in and around the community at Cibecue and within this area have recorded the Western Apache names of 296 locations; it is, to say the least, a region densely packed with place-names. But large numbers alone do not account for the high frequency with which place-names typically appear in Western Apache discourse. In part, this pattern of recurrent use results from the fact that Apaches, who travel a great deal to and from their homes, regularly call on each other to describe their trips in detail. Almost invariably, and in marked contrast to comparable reports delivered by Anglos living at Cibecue, these descriptions focus as much on *where* events occurred as on the nature and consequences of the events themselves. This practice has been observed in other Apachean groups as well, including, as Harry Hoijer noted, the Navajo: "Even the most minute occurrences are described by Navajos in close conjunction with their physical settings, suggesting that unless narrated events are spatially anchored their significance is somehow reduced and cannot be properly assessed" (personal communication, 1973). Hoijer could just as well be speaking of the Western Apache.

Something else contributes to the common use of place-names in Western Apache communities, however, and that, quite simply, is that Apaches enjoy using them. Several years ago, for example, when I was stringing a barbed-wire fence with two Apache cowboys from Cibecue, I noticed that one of them was talking quietly to himself. When I listened carefully, I discovered that he was reciting a list of place-names—a long list, punctuated only by spurts of tobacco juice, that went on for nearly ten minutes. Later, when I ventured to ask him about it, he said he "talked names" all the time. Why? "I like to,"

he said. "I ride that way in my mind." And on dozens of other occasions when I have been working or traveling with Apaches, they have
taken satisfaction in pointing out particular locations and pronouncing
their names—once, twice, three times or more. Why? "Because we
like to," or "Because those names are good to say." More often, however, Apaches account for their enthusiastic use of place-names by
commenting on the precision with which the names depict their referents. "That place looks just like its name," someone will explain, or
"That name makes me see that place like it really is." Or, as Benson
Lewis stated so succinctly, "Its name is like a picture."

Statements such as these may be interpreted in light of certain facts
about the linguistic structure of Western Apache place-names. To begin
with, it is essential to understand that all but a very few Apache place-
names take the form of complete sentences. This is made possible by
one of the most prominent components of the Western Apache language: an elaborate system of prefixes that operate most extensively
and productively to modify the stems of verbs. Thus, well-formed
sentences can be constructed that are extremely compact yet semanti-
cally very rich. It is this combination of brevity and expressiveness, I
believe, that appeals to Apaches and makes the mere pronunciation of
place-names a satisfying experience.

By way of illustration, consider the following place-names, which
have been segmented into their gross morphological constituents.

Tséé Biká' Tú Yaahiḷíné: *Tséé* (rock, stone) + *Biká'* (on top
of it; a flattish object) + *Tú* (water) + *Yaa-* (downward) + *-hi-*
(linear succession of regularly repeated movements) + *-ḷí-*
(it flows) + *-né* (the one).

   Translation: Water Flows Down On A Succession Of Flat Rocks

T'iis Bitł'áh Tú 'Oḷíné: *T'iis* (cottonwood tree) + *Bitł'áh*
(below it, underneath it) + *Tú* (water) + *'O-* (inward) + *-ḷí*
(it flows) + *-né* (the one).

   Translation: Water Flows Inward Under A Cottonwood Tree

Tséé Hadigaiyé: *Tséé* (rock, stone) + *Ha-* (up and out) + *-di-*
(extends in a line) + *-gai-* (white, whiteness) + *-yé* (the one).

   Translation: Line Of White Rocks Extends Up And Out

Notice how thoroughly descriptive these place-names are and how pointedly specific in the physical details they pick out. The names presented here are not unique in this respect. On the contrary, as we have seen, descriptive specificity is characteristic of many Western Apache place-names, and it is this distinctive attribute that causes Apaches to liken place-names to pictures and to comment appreciatively on the capacity of place-names to evoke full and accurate images of the locations to which they refer.

But why this interest in faithful evocation? The reasons, no doubt, are multiple, but one of them is closely linked to the stylistic functions served by place-names in Western Apache storytelling. Place-names are used in all forms of Apache storytelling as situating devices, as conventionalized verbal instruments for locating narrated events at and in the physical settings where the events occurred. Thus, instead of describing these settings discursively, an Apache storyteller can simply employ their names, and Apache listeners, whether they have visited the sites or not, are able to imagine in some detail how they might appear. In this way, to borrow Hoijer's felicitous phrase, narrated events are "spatially anchored" at points on the land, and the evocative pictures presented by Western Apache place-names become indispensable resources for the storyteller's craft.[4]

"All These Places Have Stories"

When I return to Cibecue in the spring of 1981, Nick Thompson is recovering from a bad case of the flu. He is weak, despondent, and uncomfortable. We speak very little and make no mention of place-names. His wife is worried about him and so am I. Within a week, however, Nick's eldest son comes to my camp with a message: I am to visit his father and bring with me two packs of Salem cigarettes and a dozen chocolate-covered doughnuts. This is good news.

When I arrive at the old man's camp, he is sitting under the cotton-wood tree by his house. A blanket is draped across his knees and he is wearing a heavy plaid jacket and a red vinyl cap with white fur-lined earflaps. There is color in his cheeks and the sparkle is back in his eyes. Shortly after we start to converse, and apropos of nothing I can discern, Nick announces that in 1931 he had sexual intercourse eight times in one night. He wants to know if I have ever been so fortunate. His wife, who has brought us each a cup of coffee, hears this remark and tells him he is a crazy old man. Nick laughs loudly. Plainly, he is feeling better.

Eventually, I ask Nick if he is ready to resume our work together. "Yes," he says, "but no more on names." What then? "Stories," is his reply. "All these places have stories. We shoot each other with them, like arrows. Come back tomorrow morning." Puzzled once again, but suspecting that the old man has a plan he wants to follow, I tell him I will return. We then discuss Nick's wages. He insists that I pay him more than I did the year before as it is necessary to keep up with inflation. I agree and we settle on a larger sum. Then comes the predictable farewell joke: a fine piece of nonsense in which Nick, speaking English and imitating certain mannerisms he has come to associate with Anglo physicians, diagnoses my badly sunburned nose as an advanced case of venereal disease.[5] This time it is Nick's wife who laughs loudest.

The next day Nick begins to instruct me on aspects of Western Apache storytelling. Consulting on a regular basis with other Apaches from Cibecue as well, I pursue this topic throughout the summer.

Historical Tales

If place-names appear frequently in ordinary forms of Western Apache discourse, their use is equally conspicuous in oral narratives. It is there, in conjunction with stories Apaches tell, that we can move closer to an interpretation of native claims about the symbolic importance of geographical features and the personalized relationships that individuals may have with them. As shown in figure 2, the people of Cibecue classify 'speech' (*yat'i'*) into three major forms: 'ordinary talk' (*yat'i'*), 'prayer' (*'okąąhí*), and 'narratives' or 'stories' (*nagoldi'é*). Narratives are further classified into four major and two minor genres (see fig. 3). The major genres include 'myths' (*godiyįhgo nagoldi'é;* literally, 'to tell of holiness'), 'historical tales' (*'ágodzaahí* or *'ágodzaahí nagoldi'é;* literally, 'to tell of that which has happened'), 'sagas' (*nlt'éégo nagoldi'é;* literally, 'to tell of pleasantness'), and stories that arise in the context of 'gossip' (*ch'idii*). The minor genres, which do not concern us here, are 'Coyote stories' (*ma' highaałyú nagoldi'é;* literally, 'to tell of Coyote's travels') and 'seduction tales' (*binííbaa' nagoldi'é;* literally, 'to tell of sexual desires').

```
                        yat'i'
                       (speech)

     yat'i'            'okąąhí             nagoldi'é
  (ordinary talk)      (prayer)        (narrative; story)
```

Figure 2   *Major categories of Western Apache speech.*

Western Apaches distinguish among the major narrative genres on two basic semantic dimensions: time and purpose. Values on the temporal dimension identify in general terms when the events recounted in narratives took place, while values on the purposive dimension describe the objectives that Apache narrators typically have in recounting them (see fig. 4). Accordingly, myths deal with events that occurred 'in the beginning' (*godiyąąná'*), a time when the universe and all things within it were achieving their present form and location. Performed only by medicine men and women, myths are presented for the primary purpose of enlightenment and instruction: to explain and reaffirm the complex processes by which the known world came into existence. Historical tales recount events that took place 'long ago' (*doo'ánííná*) when the Western Apache people, having emerged from below the surface of the earth, were developing their own distinctive ways and customs. Most historical tales describe incidents that occurred prior to the coming of whitemen, but some of these stories are set in post-reservation times, which began for the Western Apache in

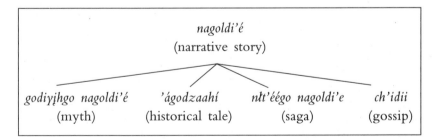

Figure 3   *Major categories of Western Apache narrative.*

Narrative Category	Temporal Locus of Events	Purpose
godiyįhgo nagoldi'é (myth)	godiyąąná' (in the beginning)	to enlighten, to instruct
'ágodzaahí (historical tale)	doo'ánííná (long ago)	to criticize, to warn, to "shoot"
nłt'éégo nagoldi'é (saga)	díijįįgo (modern times)	to entertain, to engross
ch'idii (gossip)	k'ad (now)	to inform, to malign

Figure 4 *Major categories of Western Apache narrative distinguished by temporal locus of events and primary purposes for narration.*

1872. Like myths, historical tales are intended to edify, but their main purpose is to criticize social delinquents (or, as the Apaches say, to "shoot" them), thereby impressing these individuals with the undesirability of improper behavior and alerting them to the punitive consequences of further misconduct.

Although sagas deal with historical themes, these narratives are chiefly concerned with events that have taken place in 'modern times' (díijįįgo), usually within the last sixty or seventy years. In contrast to historical tales, which focus on serious and disturbing matters, sagas are largely devoid of them. Rather than serving as vehicles of personal criticism, the primary purpose of sagas is to provide their listeners with relaxation and entertainment. Stories of the kind associated with gossip consist of reports in which persons relate and interpret events involving other members of the Western Apache community. These stories, which embrace incidents occurring 'now' or 'at present' (k'ad), are often told for no other reason than to keep people informed of local developments. Not uncommonly, however, narratives in gossip are also used to ridicule and malign the character of their subjects.

Nowhere do place-names serve more important communicative functions than in the context of historical tales. As if to accentuate this fact, stories of the *'ágodzaahí* genre are stylistically quite simple. Historical tales require no specialized lexicon, display no unusual syntactical constructions, and involve no irregular morphophonemic alternations; neither are they characterized by unique patterns of stress, pitch, volume, or intonation. In these ways, *'ágodzaahí* narratives contrast sharply with myths and sagas, which entail the use of a variety of genre-specific stylistic devices. Historical tales also differ from myths and sagas by virtue of their brevity. Whereas myths and sagas may take hours to complete, historical tales can usually be delivered in less than five minutes. Western Apache storytellers point out that this is both fitting and effective, because *'ágodzaahí* stories, like the arrows they are commonly said to represent, work best when they move swiftly. Finally, and most significantly of all, historical tales are distinguished from all other forms of Apache narrative by an opening and closing line that identifies with a place-name where the events in the narrative occurred. These lines frame the narrative, mark it unmistakably as belonging to the *'ágodzaahí* genre, and evoke a particular physical setting in which listeners can imaginatively situate everything that happens. It is hardly surprising, then, that while Apache storytellers agree that historical tales are "about" the events recounted in the tales, they also emphasize that the tales are "about" the sites at which the events took place.

If the style of Western Apache historical tales is relatively unremarkable, their content is just the opposite. Without exception, and usually in very graphic terms, historical tales focus on persons who suffer misfortune as the consequence of actions that violate Apache standards for acceptable social behavior. More specifically, *'ágodzaahí* stories tell of persons who have acted unthinkingly and impulsively in open disregard for 'Apache custom' (*ndee bi 'at'ee'*) and who pay for their transgressions by being humiliated, ostracized, or killed. Stories of the *'ágodzaahí* variety are morality tales pure and simple, and when viewed as such by the Apaches—as compact commentaries on what should be avoided so as to deal successfully and effectively with other people—they are highly informative. For what these narratives assert—

tacitly, perhaps, but with dozens of compelling examples—is that immoral behavior is irrevocably a community affair and that persons who behave badly will be punished sooner or later. Thus, just as *'ágodzaahí* stories are "about" historical events and their geographical locations, they are also "about" the system of rules and values according to which Apaches expect each other to organize and regulate their lives. In an even more fundamental sense, then, historical tales are "about" what it means to be a Western Apache, or, to make the point less dramatically, what it is that being an Apache should normally and properly entail.

To see how this is so, let us consider the texts of three historical tales and examine the manner in which they have been interpreted by their Apache narrators.

> It happened at T'iis Cho Naasikaadé (Big Cottonwood Trees Stand Here And There).
>
> Long ago, the Pimas and Apaches were fighting. The Pimas were carrying long clubs made from mesquite wood; they were also heavy and hard. Before dawn the Pimas arrived at Cibecue and attacked the Apaches there. The Pimas attacked while the Apaches were still asleep. The Pimas killed the Apaches with their clubs. An old woman woke up. She heard the Apaches crying out. The old woman thought it was her son-in-law because he often picked on her daughter. The old woman cried out: "You pick on my child a lot. You should act pleasantly toward her." Because the old woman cried out, the Pimas learned where she was. The Pimas came running to the old woman's camp and killed her with their clubs. A young girl ran away from there and hid beneath some bushes. She alone survived.
>
> It happened at Big Cottonwood Trees Stand Here And There.

Narrated by Annie Peaches, this historical tale deals with the harmful consequences that may come to persons who overstep traditional role boundaries. During the first year of marriage it is customary for young Apache couples to live in the camp of the bride's parents. At this time, the bride's mother may request that her son-in-law perform various tasks and she may also instruct and criticize him. Later, however, when the couple establishes a separate residence, the bride's mother forfeits this right and may properly interfere in her son-in-law's affairs only at the request of her daughter. Mrs. Peaches explains that women who do not abide by this arrangement imply that their sons-in-law are immature and irresponsible, which is a source of acute embarrassment for the young men and their wives. Thus, even when meddling might seem to serve a useful purpose, it should be scrupulously avoided. The woman on whom this story centers failed to remember this and was instantly killed.

It happened at Tséé Chiizh Dah Sidilé (Coarse-Textured Rocks Lie Above In A Compact Cluster).

Long ago, a man became sexually attracted to his stepdaughter. He was living below Coarse-Textured Rocks Lie Above In A Compact Cluster with his stepdaughter and her mother. Waiting until no one else was present, and sitting alone with her, he started to molest her. The girl's maternal uncle happened to come by and he killed the man with a rock. The man's skull was cracked open. It was raining. The girl's maternal uncle dragged the man's body up above to Coarse-Textured Rocks Lie Above In A Compact Cluster and placed it there in a storage pit. The girl's mother came home and was told by her daughter of all that had happened. The people who owned the storage pit removed the man's body and put it somewhere else. The people never had a wake for the dead man's body.

It happened at Coarse-Textured Rocks Lie Above In A Compact Cluster.

Narrated by Benson Lewis, this historical tale deals with the crime of incest, for sexual contact with stepchildren is considered by Western Apaches to be an incestuous act. According to Mr. Lewis, the key line in the story is the penultimate one in which he observes, "The people never had a wake for the dead man's body." We may assume, Lewis says, that because the dead man's camp was located near the storage pit in which his body was placed, the people who owned the pit were also his relatives. This makes the neglect with which his corpse was treated all the more profound, since kinspeople are bound by the strongest of obligations to care for each other when they die. That the dead man's relatives chose to dispense with customary mortuary ritual shows with devastating clarity that they wished to disown him completely.

It happened at Ndee Dah Naazįné (Men Stand Above Here And There).

Long ago, a man killed a cow off the reservation. The cow belonged to a whiteman. The man was arrested by a policeman living at Cibecue at Men Stand Above Here And There. The policeman was an Apache. The policeman took the man to the head army officer at Fort Apache. There, at Fort Apache, the head army officer questioned him. "What do you want?" he said. The policeman said, "I need cartridges and food." The policeman said nothing about the man who had killed the whiteman's cow. That night some people spoke to the policeman. "It is best to report on him," they said to him. The next day the policeman returned to the head army officer. "Now what do you want?" he said. The policeman said, "Yesterday I was going to say HELLO and GOOD-BYE but I forgot to do it." Again he said nothing about the man he arrested. Someone was working with words on his mind. The policeman returned with the man to Cibecue. He released him at Men Stand Above Here And There.

It happened at Men Stand Above Here And There.

This story, narrated by Nick Thompson, describes what happened to an Apache who acted too much like a whiteman. Between 1872 and 1895, when the Western Apaches were strictly confined to their reservations by U.S. military forces, disease and malnutrition took the lives of many people. Consequently, Apaches who listen to this historical tale find it perfectly acceptable that the man who lived at Men Stand Above Here And There should have killed and butchered a whiteman's cow. What is not acceptable is that the policeman, another Apache from the same settlement, should have arrested the rustler and contemplated taking him to jail. But the policeman's plans were thwarted. Someone used witchcraft on him and made him stupid and forgetful. He never informed the military officer at Fort Apache of the real purpose of his visit, and his second encounter with the officer—in which he apologized for neglecting to say "hello" and "good-bye" the previous day—revealed him to be an absurd and laughable figure. Although Western Apaches find portions of this story amusing, Nick Thompson explains that they understand it first and foremost as a harsh indictment of persons who join with outsiders against members of their own community and who, as if to flaunt their lack of allegiance, parade the attitudes and mannerisms of whitemen.

So far my remarks on what Western Apache historical tales are "about" have centered on features of textual content. This is a familiar strategy and certainly a necessary one, but it is also incomplete. In addition to everything else—places, events, moral standards, conceptions of cultural identity—every historical tale is also "about" the person at whom it is directed. This is because the telling of a historical tale is almost always prompted by an individual's having committed one or more social offenses to which the act of narration, together with the tale itself, is intended as a critical and remedial response. Thus, on occasions when 'ágodzaahí stories are actually told—by real Apache storytellers, in real interpersonal contexts, to real social offenders—these narratives are understood to be accompanied by an unstated message from the storyteller that may be phrased something like this: "I know that you have acted in a way similar or analogous to the way in which someone acted in the story I am telling you. If you continue to act in this way, something similar or analogous to what has happened to the character in the story might also happen to you." This metacommunicative message is just as important as any conveyed by the text of the storyteller's tale. For Apaches contend that if the message is taken to heart by the person at whom the tale is aimed— and if, in conjunction with lessons drawn from the tale itself, he or she resolves to improve his or her behavior—a lasting bond will have been created between that individual and the site or sites at which events in the tale took place. The cultural premises that inform this powerful idea will be made explicit presently; but first, in order to understand more clearly what the idea involves, let us examine the circumstances that led to the telling of a historical tale at Cibecue and see how this narrative affected the person for whom it was told.

In early June 1977, a seventeen-year-old Apache woman attended a girls' puberty ceremonial at Cibecue with her hair rolled up in a set of pink plastic curlers. She had returned home two days before from a boarding school in Utah where this sort of ornamentation was considered fashionable by her peers. Something so mundane would have gone unnoticed by others were it not for the fact that Western Apache women of all ages are expected to appear at puberty ceremonials with their hair worn loose. This is one of several ways that women have of showing respect for the ceremonial and also, by implication, for the people who have staged it. The practice of presenting oneself with free-flowing hair is also understood to contribute to the ceremonial's effectiveness, for Apaches hold that the ritual's most basic objectives, which are to invest the pubescent girl with qualities necessary for life as an adult, cannot be achieved unless standard forms of respect are faithfully observed. On this occasion at Cibecue, everyone was following custom except the young woman who arrived wearing curlers. She soon became an object of attention and quiet expressions of disapproval, but no one spoke to her about the cylindrical objects in her hair.

Two weeks later, the same young woman made a large stack of tortillas and brought them to the camp of her maternal grandmother, a widow in her mid-sixties who had organized a small party to celebrate the birthday of her eldest grandson. Eighteen people were on hand, myself included, and all of us were treated to hot coffee and a dinner of boiled beef and potatoes. When the meal was over, casual conversation began to flow, and the young woman seated herself on the ground next to her younger sister. And then—quietly, deftly, and quite without warning—her grandmother narrated a version of the historical tale about the forgetful Apache policeman who behaved too much like a whiteman. Shortly after the story was finished, the young woman stood up, turned away wordlessly, and walked off in the direction of her home. Uncertain of what had happened, I asked her grandmother why she had departed. Had the young woman suddenly become ill? "No," her grandmother replied. "I shot her with an arrow."

Approximately two years after this incident occurred, I found myself in the company of the young woman with the taste for distinctive hairstyles. She had purchased a large carton of groceries at the trading post at Cibecue, and when I offered to drive her home with them she accepted. I inquired on the way if she remembered the time that her grandmother had told us the story about the forgetful policeman. She said she did and then went on, speaking in English, to describe her reactions to it. "I think maybe my grandmother was getting after me, but then I think maybe not, maybe she's working on somebody else. Then I think back on that dance and I know it's me for sure. I sure don't like how she's talking about me, so I quit looking like that. I threw those curlers away." In order to reach the young woman's camp, we had to pass within a few hundred yards of Men Stand Above Here And There, the place where the man had lived who was arrested for rustling in the story. I pointed it out to my companion. She said nothing for several moments. Then she smiled and spoke softly in her own language: "I know that place. It stalks me every day."

The comments of this Western Apache woman on her experience as the target of a historical tale are instructive in several respects. To begin with, her statement enables us to imagine something of the sizable psychological impact that historical tales may have on the persons to whom they are presented. Then, too, we can see how *'ágodzaahí* stories may produce quick and palpable effects on the behavior of such individuals, causing them to modify their social conduct in quite specific ways. Last, and most revealing of all, the young woman's remarks provide a clear illustration of what Apaches have in mind when they assert that historical tales may establish highly meaningful relationships between individuals and features of the natural landscape.

To appreciate fully the significance of these relationships, as well as their influence on the lives of Western Apache people, we must explore more thoroughly the manner in which the relationships are conceptualized. This can be accomplished through a closer examination of Apache ideas about the activity of storytelling and the acknowledged power of oral narratives, especially historical tales, to promote beneficial changes in people's attitudes toward their responsibilities as members of a moral community. These ideas, which combine to form a native model of how oral narratives work to achieve their intended effects, are expressed in terms of a single dominant metaphor. By now it should come as no surprise to learn that the metaphor draws heavily on the imagery of hunting.

Stalking with Stories

Nick Thompson is tired. We have been talking about hunting with stories for two days now and the old man has not had an easy time of it. Yesterday, my uneven control of the Western Apache language prevented him from speaking as rapidly and eloquently as he would have liked, and on too many occasions I was forced to interrupt him with questions. At one point, bored and annoyed with my queries, he told me that I reminded him of a horsefly buzzing around his head. Later, however, when he was satisfied that I could follow at least the outline of his thoughts, he recorded on tape a lengthy statement which he said contained everything he wanted me to know. "Take it with you and listen to it," he said. "Tomorrow we put it in English." For the past six hours that is what we have been trying to do. We are finished now and weary of talking. In the weeks to come I will worry about the depth and force of our translation, and twice more I will return to Nick's camp with other questions. But the hardest work is over and both of us know it. Nick has taught me already that hunting with stories is not a simple matter, and as I prepare to leave I say so. "We know," he says, and that is all. Here is Nick Thompson's statement:

> This is what we know about our stories. They go to work on your mind and make you think about your life. Maybe you've not been acting right. Maybe you've been stingy. Maybe you've been chasing after women. Maybe you've been trying to act like a whiteman. People don't *like* it! So someone goes hunting for you—maybe your grandmother, your grandfather, your uncle. It doesn't matter. Anyone can do it.
>
> So someone stalks you and tells a story about what happened long ago. It doesn't matter if other people are around—you're going to know he's aiming that story at you. All of a sudden it *hits* you! It's like an arrow, they say. Sometimes it just bounces off—it's too soft and you don't

think about anything. But when it's strong it goes in deep and starts working on your mind right away. No one says anything to you, only that story is all, but now you know that people have been watching you and talking about you. They don't like how you've been acting. So you have to think about your life.

Then you feel weak, real weak, like you are sick. You don't want to eat or talk to anyone. That story is working on you now. You keep thinking about it. That story is changing you now, making you want to live right. That story is making you want to replace yourself. You think only of what you did that was wrong and you don't like it. So you want to live better. After a while, you don't like to think of what you did wrong. So you try to forget that story. You try to pull that arrow out. You think it won't hurt anymore because now you want to live right.

It's hard to keep on living right. Many things jump up at you and block your way. But you won't forget that story. You're going to see the place where it happened, maybe every day if it's nearby and close to Cibecue. If you don't see it, you're going to hear its name and see it in your mind. It doesn't matter if you get old—that place will keep on stalking you like the one who shot you with the story. Maybe that person will die. Even so, that place will keep on stalking you. It's like that person is still alive.

Even if we go far away from here to some big city, places around here keep stalking us. If you live wrong, you will hear the names and see the places in your mind. They keep on stalking you, even if you go across oceans. The names of all these places are good. They make you remember how to live right, so you want to replace yourself again.

A Western Apache Hunting Metaphor

Nick Thompson's model of Western Apache storytelling is a compelling construction. To be sure, it is the formulation of one Apache only; but it is fully explicit and amply detailed, and I have been able to corroborate almost every aspect of it with other Apaches from

Cibecue. This is not to imply that all Apache people interpret their hunting metaphor for storytelling in exactly the same fashion. On the contrary, one of the properties of any successful metaphor is that it can be refined and enlarged in different ways. Thus, some Apaches assert that historical tales, like arrows, leave wounds—mental and emotional wounds—and that the process of "replacing oneself" is properly understood as a form of healing. Other Apache consultants stress that place-names, rather than the sites to which the names refer, are what individuals are unable to forget after historical tales have done their work. But differences and elaborations of this kind only demonstrate the scope and flexibility of the hunting metaphor and do nothing to alter its basic contours or to diminish its considerable force. Neither does such variation reduce in any way the utility of the metaphor as an effective instrument of Western Apache thought.

Although I cannot claim to understand the full range of meanings that the hunting model for storytelling has for Western Apache people, the general premises on which the model rests seem clear to me. Historical tales have the capacity to thrust socially delinquent persons into periods of intense critical self-examination from which (ideally, at least) they emerge chastened, repentant, and determined to "live right." Simultaneously, people who have been "shot" with stories experience a form of anguish—shame, guilt, perhaps only pervasive chagrin—that moves them to alter aspects of their behavior so as to conform more closely to community expectations. In short, historical tales have the power to change people's ideas about themselves: to force them to admit to social failings, to dwell seriously on the significance of these lapses, and to resolve, it is hoped once and for all, not to repeat them. As Nick Thompson says, historical tales "make you think about your life."

After stories and storytellers have served this beneficial purpose, features of the physical landscape take over and perpetuate it. Mountains and arroyos step in symbolically for grandmothers and uncles. Just as the latter have "stalked" delinquent individuals in the past, so, too, particular locations continue to stalk them in the present. Such surveillance is essential, Apaches maintain, because "living right" requires constant care and attention, and there is always a possibility that old stories and their initial impact, like old arrows and their wounds, will fade and disappear. In other words, there is always a chance that persons who have "replaced themselves" once—or twice, or three times—will relax their guard against "badness" and slip back into undesirable forms of social conduct. Consequently, Apaches explain, individuals need to be continuously reminded of why they were "shot" in the first place and how they reacted to it at the time. Geographical sites, together with the crisp mental pictures of them presented by their names, serve admirably in this capacity, inviting people to recall their earlier failings and encouraging them to resolve, once again, to avoid them in the future. Grandmothers and uncles must perish, but the landscape endures, and for this the Apache people are grateful. "The land," Nick Thompson observes, "looks after us. The land keeps badness away."

It should now be possible for the reader to interpret the Western Apache texts at the beginning of this essay in a manner roughly compatible with the Apache ideas that have shaped them. Moreover, he or she should be able to appreciate that the claims put forward in the texts are reasonable and appropriate, credible and "correct," the principled expressions of an underlying logic that invests them with internal consistency and coherent conceptual structure. As we have seen, this structure is supplied in large part by the hunting metaphor for Western Apache storytelling. It is chiefly in accordance with this metaphor—or, more exactly, in accordance with the symbolic associations it orders and makes explicit—that the claims presented earlier finally make sense.

Thus, Annie Peaches's claim—that the land occupied by Western Apaches "makes the people live right"—becomes understandable as a proposition about the moral significance of geographical locations as this has been established by historical tales with which the locations are associated. Similarly, Wilson Lavender's claim—that Apaches who fail to remember place-names "forget how to be strong"—rests on an association of place-names with a belief in the power of historical tales to discourage forms of socially unacceptable behavior. Apaches also associate places and their names with the narrators of historical tales, and Benson Lewis's claim—that a certain mountain near Cibecue is his maternal grandmother—can be interpreted only in light of this assumption. The hunting metaphor for storytelling also informs Ronnie Lupe's claim that Western Apache children who are not exposed to historical tales tend to have interpersonal difficulties. As he puts it, "They don't know the stories of what happened at these places. That's why some of them get into trouble." What Mr. Lupe is claiming, of course, is that children who do not learn to associate places and their names with historical tales cannot appreciate the utility of these narratives as guidelines for dealing responsibly and amicably with other people. Consequently, he believes, such individuals are more likely than others to act in ways that run counter to Apache social norms, a sure sign that they are "losing the land."

Losing the land is something the Western Apaches can ill afford to do, for geographical features have served the people for centuries as indispensable mnemonic pegs on which to hang the moral teachings of their history. Accordingly, such locations present themselves as instances of what Mikhail Bakhtin has called *chronotopes*. As Bakhtin (1981:7) describes them, chronotopes are

> points in the geography of a community where time and space intersect and fuse. Time takes on flesh and becomes visible for human contemplation; likewise, space becomes charged and responsive to the movements of time and history and the enduring character of a people. . . . Chronotopes thus stand as monuments to the community itself, as symbols of it, as forces operating to shape its members' images of themselves.

Whether or not one is pleased with Bakhtin's use of the term *chronotope* (it is more widely known, but in a very different sense, as a concept in Albert Einstein's theory of relativity), his observations on the cultural importance of geographical landmarks apply nicely to the Western Apache. The Apache landscape is full of named locations where time and space have fused and where, through the agency of historical tales, their intersection is "made visible for human contemplation." It is also apparent that such locations, charged as they are with personal and social significance, work in important ways to shape the images that Apaches have—or should have—of themselves. Speaking to people like Nick Thompson and Ronnie Lupe, to Annie Peaches and Benson Lewis, one forms the impression that Apaches view the landscape as a repository of distilled wisdom, a stern but benevolent keeper of tradition, an ever-vigilant ally in the efforts of individuals and whole communities to maintain a set of standards for social living that is uniquely and distinctly their own. In the world that the Western Apaches have constituted for themselves, features of the landscape have become symbols of and for this way of living, the symbols of a culture and the enduring moral character of its people.

We may assume that this relationship with the land has been pervasive throughout Western Apache history, but in today's climate of social change, its importance for Apache people may well be deepening. Communities such as Cibecue, formerly isolated and very much turned inward, were opened up by paved roads less than twenty-five years ago, and the consequences of improved access and freer travel— including greatly increased contact with Anglo-Americans—have been pronounced. Younger Apaches, who today complain frequently about the tedium of village life, have started to develop new tastes and ambitions, and some of them are eager to explore the outside world. Older members of the community understand this desire and do little to try to stifle it, but they are concerned that as younger people learn more and more of the "whiteman's way" they will also lose sight of portions of their own. Let the pink plastic curlers at the girls' puberty ceremonial stand as one case in point. What can be done to guard against this unsettling possibility? Perhaps, in the long run, nothing. But for now, and probably for some time to come, the landscape is doing a respectable job. It is there, "stalking" people all the time, and to the extent that it remains not merely a physical presence but an omnipresent moral force, young Apaches are not likely to forget that the "whiteman's way" belongs to a different world.

Having pursued Western Apache ideas about the land this far, it is worth inquiring whether similar conceptions are held by other groups of American Indian people. Although ethnographic materials bearing on this question are in short supply (I identify some of the reasons for this shortage further on), there is highly reliable evidence from another source—the published work of modern Indian writers—that general similarities do exist. Consider, for example, the following statement by Leslie M. Silko, poet and novelist from the pueblo of Laguna in New Mexico. After explaining that stories "function basically as makers of our identity," Silko (1981:69) goes on to discuss Pueblo narratives in relation to the land:

> The stories cannot be separated from geographical locations, from actual physical places within the land. . . . And the stories are so much a part of these places that it is almost impossible for future generations to lose the stories because there are so many imposing geological elements . . . you cannot live in that land without asking or looking at or noticing a boulder or rock. And there's always a story.

A number of other American Indian authors, among them Vine Deloria, Jr. (Standing Rock Sioux), Simon Ortiz (Acoma), Joy Harjo (Creek), and the cultural anthropologist Alfonso Ortiz (San Juan Pueblo), have written with skill and insight about the moral dimensions of Native American conceptions of the land. No one, however, has addressed the subject with greater sensitivity than N. Scott Momaday (Kiowa). The following passages, taken from his short essay entitled "Native American Attitudes to the Environment" (1974), show clearly what is involved, not only for the Western Apache but for other tribes as well.

> You cannot understand how the Indian thinks of himself in relation to the world around him unless you understand his conception of what is appropriate; particularly what is morally appropriate within the context of that relationship. . . . (1974:82)
>
> The native American ethic with respect to the physical world is a matter of reciprocal appropriation: appropriations in which man invests himself in the landscape, and at the same time incorporates the landscape into his own most fundamental experience. . . . This appropriation is primarily a matter of imagination which is moral in kind. I mean to say that we are all, I suppose, what we imagine ourselves to be. And that is certainly true of the American Indian. . . . [The Indian] is someone who thinks of himself in a particular way and his idea comprehends his relationship to the physical world. He imagines himself in terms of that relationship and others. And it is that act of imagination, that moral act of

imagination, which constitutes his understanding of the physical world. (1974:80)

"Goodness Is All Around"

The news sweeps through Cibecue like brush fire: Nick Thompson must have purchased a wheelchair because he was seen this morning *racing* in one, against his four-year-old grandson. The little boy, shrieking with glee and running as fast as he could, won the contest, but the old man finished close behind. Nick's wife was horrified and his oldest daughter yelled twice to him to stop. But he kept on going, wheeling himself along with his one good arm and paying no attention whatsoever. That old man will do anything! He doesn't care at all what people think! And what if he *crashed!*

Nick Thompson has no intention of crashing. Seated now in his familiar place beneath the cottonwood tree near his house, he says that racing his wheelchair is perfectly safe. He says he plans to do it again; he has already challenged his six-year-old granddaughter. He says he is tired of the women in his camp telling him what to do. He is also tired of not being able to move around freely, which is why he bought the wheelchair in the first place, and people should understand this and stop making such a fuss. And besides, the old man observes, the wheelchair has good brakes. That's what he likes best— getting up speed and jamming on the brakes.

The summer of 1981 is almost gone, and soon I must leave Cibecue. I have walked to Nick's camp to tell him good-bye. This is never easy for me, and we spend most of the time talking about other things. Eventually, I move to thank him for his generosity, his patience, and the things he has taught me. Nick responds by pointing with his lips to a low ridge that runs behind his home in an easterly direction away from Cibecue Creek. "That is a good place," he says. "These are all good places. Goodness is all around."

The old man pauses. Then he reaches beneath the seat of his chair and produces a blue and white cap which he places, slightly askew, on his head. The embossed emblem in front, which is in the shape of a car, reads "Ford Racing Team." We both begin to laugh . . . and laugh and laugh.

Language and Environment

Anthropologists have long been interested in the relationships that link American Indian communities to their ecological settings. In the great majority of cases, these relationships have been described and interpreted exclusively in materialist terms; that is, in terms of demographic patterns, subsistence strategies, and forms of social organization that facilitate the exploitation of environmental resources and function in this way to assure the biological survival of native populations. While this approach is useful for certain purposes, it is clear that materialist models are one-sided and incomplete. They ignore the fact that American Indians, like groups of people everywhere, maintain a complex array of symbolic relationships with their physical surroundings and that these relationships, which may have little to do with the business of making a living, play a fundamental role in shaping other forms of social activity. What has been ignored, in other words, are the cultural instruments with which American Indians fashion understandings of their environments, the ideational resources with which they constitute their surroundings and invest them with value and significance. We need not go far to seek the reasons for this neglect. Having committed themselves to a search for statistical regularities and functional interdependencies, human ecologists are obliged to regard the semiotic dimensions of human environments as epiphenomena that lie outside the proper sphere of their concern. And so, ironically, many human ecologists have become largely uninterested in what human beings take their environments to mean. This is unfortunate because, as Mihaly Csikszentmihalyi and Edward Rochberg-Halton (1981:1) have written,

> to understand what people are and what they might become,
> one must understand what goes on between people and
> things. What things are cherished, and why, should become
> part of our knowledge of human beings. Yet it is surprising
> how little we know about what things mean to people. By and
> large social scientists have neglected a full investigation of the
> relationship between people and objects.

There is no doubt in the minds of many anthropologists, including a substantial number who have worked with American Indians, that studies in ecology have made a valuable contribution. In particular, these investigations have shown that indigenous populations may adapt with exquisite intricacy to the physical conditions of their existence (including, of course, the presence of other human populations), and that modifications in these conditions may have a range of dynamic effects on the structure and organization of social institutions. But ecological models have been consistently formulated at a "systemic" level that is well removed from the level of the individual—and it is individuals, not social institutions, who make and act on cultural meanings. Conventional ecological studies proceed on the tacit premise that what people think about the environment—how they perceive it, how they conceptualize it, or, to borrow a phrase from the ethnomethodologists, how they "actively construct" it—is basically irrelevant to an understanding of man-land relationships. To accept this premise is to conclude that cultural meanings are similarly irrelevant and that the layers of significance with which human beings blanket the environment have little bearing on how they lead their lives. But the premise is not correct, for American Indians or anyone else, and to suppose otherwise would be a serious mistake.

Accordingly, and by way of illustration, I have attempted to show here that Western Apache conceptions of the land work in specific ways to influence Apaches' conceptions of themselves, and vice versa, and that the two together work to influence patterns of social action. To reject this possibility—or, as many ecologists would be inclined to do, to rule it out a priori as inconsequential—would have the effect of "removing" the Apaches from the world as they have constructed it. This, in turn, would obliterate all aspects of their moral relationship with the land. For reasons that should now be apparent, this relationship is crucial to Apaches—quite as crucial, I expect, as any that deals with subsistence or economics—and for us to lose sight of it could only have damaging consequences.

Societies must survive, but social life is more than just surviving. And cultural meanings are epiphenomenal only for those who choose to make them so. I would like to witness the development of a cultural ecology that is cultural in the fullest sense, a broader and more flexible approach to the study of man-land relationships in which the symbolic properties of environmental phenomena receive the same kind of attention that has traditionally been given to their material counterparts. The Western Apaches of Cibecue understand their land, and act on their understandings of it, in ways that standard ecological approaches would overlook. Does this mean that such understandings are unimportant for the Western Apache? For a stronger and more rounded anthropology? I suggest that on both counts it does not.

Cultural constructions of the environment, whether those of American Indians or of peoples elsewhere in the world, will remain largely inaccessible unless we are prepared to sit down and listen to our native consultants talk—not only about landscapes, which of course we must do, but about talking about landscapes as well. And since spatial conceptions, like temporal ones, are so often found expressed in figurative language, this is almost certain to lead to a consideration of metaphor. Paul Radin (1916:137), writing some years ago of the Winnebago Indians of the Great Lakes, described a particular case that is probably typical of many others:

> Ideas about the habitat are frequently set forth in elaborate
> similes and metaphors which equate disparate objects in a
> fashion that at first seems quite unfathomable. Yet once these
> tropes are uncovered, it can be seen that they rest upon firm
> assumptions about the workings of nature which, though
> different from our own, fit together intelligibly.

George Lakoff and Mark Johnson (1980:1) have stated that the essence of metaphor is "understanding and experiencing one kind of thing in terms of another." Although this definition departs relatively little from the classical one given by Aristotle ("metaphor implies an intuitive perception of the similarity in dissimilars"), it points to a problem in the study of language and culture that is deeply ethnographic. For where metaphor is concerned, the question always arises, On what *grounds* is one kind of thing understood in terms of another? In other words, what must individuals believe about themselves and their surroundings for their metaphors to "work"?

This question focuses attention on the large body of implicit cultural assumptions that the members of any speech community rely on to interpret instances of situated discourse. Such assumptions, which

have been variously described as comprising a speaker's "presuppositions," "background knowledge," or "beliefs about the world," present
difficulties for all theories of language that seek to restrict the idea of
linguistic competence to a speaker's tacit knowledge of grammatical
rules. Metaphor threatens both the validity of this distinction and the
utility of maintaining it, because the ability to interpret even the simplest forms of metaphorical speech cannot be accounted for with grammatical rules alone; presuppositions are also fundamentally involved.
This is clearly illustrated by Nick Thompson's statement on the Western Apache hunting metaphor for storytelling. As he explicates the
metaphor, thereby enabling us to interpret a set of claims that Apaches
have made, he articulates the cultural assumptions that make these claims
possible in the first place. In other words, he makes presuppositions
explicit. Storytellers are hunters for the Western Apache—and stories,
arrows; and mountains, grandmothers—by virtue of shared beliefs
about the world. Culturally wrought and culturally specific, such beliefs provide the conceptual materials with which competent Apache
speakers locate the similarities in metaphorical dissimilars and, in doing so, experience one kind of thing in terms of another. Such beliefs
make their metaphors "work."

What all of this implies (obviously for many anthropologists, less
so for many linguists) is that grasping other peoples' metaphors requires ethnography as much as it does linguistics. Unless we pursue
the two together, the full extent to which metaphorical structures influence patterns of thought and action is likely to elude us. "To inhabit a language," Samuel Johnson wrote, "is to inhabit a living
universe, and vice-versa." That "vice versa" is critical because it suggests, correctly I believe, that linguistics and ethnography are integral
parts of the same basic enterprise, one of whose purposes is to construct principled interpretations of culturally constituted worlds and
to try to understand what living in them is like. If anthropology stands
to benefit from an approach to cultural ecology that attends more
closely to the symbolic forms with which human environments are
perceived and rendered significant, so, too, there is a need for an
expanded view of linguistic competence in which beliefs about the
world occupy a central place. If it is the meaning of things that we are

after—the meanings of words, objects, events, and the claims people make about themselves—language and culture must be studied hand in hand. Our knowledge of one can only enhance our knowledge of the other.

"We Know It Happened"

If the thoughts presented here have a measure of theoretical interest, recent experience persuades me that they can have practical value as well. During the past decade I have written a number of documents for use in litigation concerning the settlement of Western Apache water rights in the state of Arizona. Until a final decision is reached in the case, I am not permitted to describe the contents of these documents in detail, but one of my assignments has been to write a report dealing with Apache conceptions of the physical environment. That report contains sections on Western Apache place-names, oral narratives, and certain metaphors that Apache people use to formulate aspects of their relationship with the land.

Preliminary hearings resulted in a judgment favorable to Apache interests; apparently my report was useful, mainly because it helped to pave the way for testimony by native witnesses. One of these witnesses was Nick Thompson, and according to attorneys on both sides, the old man's appearance had a decisive impact. After Nick had taken his place on the stand, he was asked by an attorney why he considered water to be important to his people. A man of eminent good sense, Nick replied, "Because we drink it!" And then, without missing a beat, he launched into a historical tale about a large spring not far from Cibecue—Tú Nchaa Halíné (Much Water Flows Up And Out)—where long ago a man was mysteriously drowned after badly mistreating his wife. When Nick finished the story he went on to say: "We know it happened, so we know not to act like that man who died. It's good we have that water. We need it to live. It's good we have that spring too. We need it to live right." Then the old man smiled to himself and his eyes began to dance.

Speaking with Names

What we call the landscape is generally considered to be something "out there."
But, while some aspects of the landscape are clearly external to both our bodies and
our minds, what each of us actually experiences is selected, shaped, and colored by
what we know.
—Barrie Greenbie, Spaces: Dimensions of the Human Landscape

An unfamiliar landscape, like an unfamiliar language, is always a little daunting, and when the two are encountered together—as they are, commonly enough, in those out-of-the-way communities where ethnographers tend to crop up—the combination may be downright unsettling. From the outset, of course, neither landscape nor language can be ignored. On the contrary, the shapes and colors and contours of the land, together with the shifting sounds and cadences of native discourse, thrust themselves upon the newcomer with a force so vivid and direct as to be virtually inescapable. Yet for all their sensory immediacy (and there are occasions, as any ethnographer will attest, when the sheer constancy of it grows to formidable proportions) landscape and discourse seem resolutely out of reach. Although close at hand and tangible in the extreme, each in its own way appears remote and inaccessible, anonymous and indistinct, and somehow, implausibly, a shade less than fully believable. And neither landscape nor discourse, as if determined to accentuate these conflicting impressions, may seem the least bit interested in having them resolved. Emphatically "there" but conspicuously lacking in accustomed forms of order and arrangement, landscape and discourse confound the stranger's efforts to invest them with significance, and this uncommon predicament, which produces nothing if not uncertainty, can be keenly disconcerting.

Surrounded by foreign geographical objects and intractable acts of speech, even the most practiced ethnographer becomes diffident and cautious. For the meanings of objects and acts alike can only be guessed at, and once the guesses have been recognized for the arbitrary constructions they almost always are, one senses acutely that one's own experience of things and events "out there" cannot be used as a reliable guide to the experience of native people. In other words, one must acknowledge that local understandings of external realities are fashioned from local cultural materials, and that, knowing little or nothing of the latter, one's ability to make appropriate sense of "what is" and "what occurs" in another's environment is bound to be deficient. For better or worse, the ethnographer sees, landscape and speech acts do not interpret their own significance. Initially at least, and typically for many months to come, this is a task that only members of the indigenous community are adequately equipped to accomplish; and accomplish it they do, day in and day out, with enviably little difficulty. For where native men and women are concerned, the external world *is* as it appears to them to be—naturally, unproblematically, and more or less consistently—and rarely do they have reason to consider that the coherence it displays is an intricate product of their own collective manufacture. Cultures run deep, as the saying goes, and all of us take our "native's point of view" very much for granted.

In this way, or something roughly like it, the ethnographer comes to appreciate that features of the local landscape, no less than utterances exchanged in forms of daily discourse, acquire value and significance by virtue of the ideational systems with which they are apprehended and construed. Symbolically constituted, socially transmitted, and individually applied, such systems operate to place flexible constraints on how the physical environment can (and should) be known, how its occupants can (and should) be found to act, and how the doings of both can (and should) be discerned to affect each other. Accordingly, each system delineates a distinctive way of being-in-the-world (Ricoeur 1979), an informal logic for engaging the world and thinking about the engagement (Geertz 1973), an array of conceptual frameworks for organizing experience and rendering it intelligible (Goffman 1974). In any community, the meanings assigned to geographical features and acts of speech will be influenced by the subjective determinations of the people who assign them, and these determinations, needless to say, will exhibit variation. But the character of the meanings—their steadier themes, their recurrent tonalities, and, above all, their conventionalized modes of expression—will bear the stamp of a common cast of mind. Constructions of reality that reflect conceptions of reality, the meanings of landscapes and acts of speech are personalized manifestations of a shared perspective on the human condition.

Mulling over these apparent truths, the ethnographer is likely to notice that members of the local community involve themselves with their geographical landscape in at least three distinct ways. First, they may simply observe the landscape, attending for reasons of their own to aspects of its appearance and to sundry goings-on within it. Second, they may use the landscape, engaging in a broad range of physical activities which, depending on their duration and extent, may leave portions of the landscape visibly modified. Third, native people may communicate about the landscape, formulating descriptions and other representations of it that they share in the course of social gatherings. On many occasions, community members can be observed to alternate freely among these different modes of involvement (they may also, of course, combine them), but it is obvious that events in the last mode—communicative acts of topographic representation—will be most revealing of the conceptual instruments with which native people interpret their natural surroundings. And though such representations may be fashioned from a variety of semiotic materials (gestural, pictorial, musical, and others), few are more instructive than those which are wrought with words.

Ordinary talk, the ethnographer sees, provides a readily available window onto the structure and significance of other peoples' worlds, and so (slowly at first, by fits and starts, and never without protracted bouts of guessing) he or she begins to learn to listen. And also to freshly see. For as native concepts and beliefs find external purchase on specific features of the local topography, the entire landscape acquires a crisp new dimension that seems to move it more surely into view. What earlier appeared as a circular sweep of undifferentiated natural architecture now starts to emerge as a precise arrangement of named sites and localities, each distinguished by a set of physical attributes and cultural associations that mark it as unique. In native discourse, the local landscape falls neatly and repeatedly into *places*—and places, as Franz Boas (1934) emphasized some years ago, are social constructions par excellence.

It is excessive to claim, as George Trager (1968:537) has done, that "the way man talks about the physical universe is his only way of knowing anything about it." Nonetheless, most ethnographers would agree that Trager's claim contains a large amount of truth, and some have suggested that this can be seen with particular clarity where language and landscapes are concerned. For whenever the members of a community speak about their landscape—whenever they name it, or classify it, or tell stories about it—they unthinkingly represent it in ways that are compatible with shared understandings of how, in the fullest sense, they know themselves to occupy it. Which is simply to note that in conversational encounters, brief and lengthy alike, individuals exchange accounts and observations of the landscape that consistently presuppose mutually held ideas of what it actually is, why its constituent places are important, and how it may intrude on the practical affairs of its inhabitants. Thus, if frequently by implication and allusion only, bits and pieces of a common worldview are given situated relevance and made temporarily accessible. In talk about the landscape, as Martin Heidegger (1977:323) so aptly put it, cultural conceptions of "dwelling together" are placed on oblique display.

At the same time, however, and often just as obliquely, persons who engage in this sort of talk also exchange messages about aspects of the social encounter in which they are jointly involved, including their framings of the encounter itself (i.e., "what is going on here") and their morally guided assessments of the comportment of fellow participants. Consequently, the possibility arises that as speakers communicate about the landscape and the kinds of dealings they have with it, they may also communicate about themselves as social actors and the kinds of dealings they are having with one another. Stated more precisely, statements pertaining to the landscape may be employed to convey tacit messages about the organization of face-to-face relationships and the normative footings on which those relationships are currently being conducted. Indirectly perhaps, but tellingly all the same, participants in verbal encounters thus put their landscapes to work—interactional work—and how they choose to go about it may shed interesting light on matters other than geography. For example, when a character in a short story by Paul Gallico (1954:69) says to his chronically unfaithful lover, "Go make a nest on Forty-Second Street," it is altogether clear that he is drawing upon the cultural meaning of a place to communicate something important about their relationship.

From the standpoint of the ethnographer, then, situated talk of geographical landscapes is more than a valuable resource for exploring local conceptions of the surrounding material universe. It may, in addition, be useful for interpreting forms of social action that regularly occur within that universe. For landscapes are always available to their seasoned inhabitants in more than material terms. Landscapes are available in symbolic terms as well, and so, chiefly through the manifold agencies of speech, they can be "detached" from their fixed spatial moorings and transformed into instruments of thought and vehicles of purposive behavior. Thus transformed, landscapes and the places that fill them become tools for the imagination, expressive means for accomplishing verbal deeds, and also, of course, eminently portable possessions to which individuals can maintain deep and abiding attachments, regardless of where they travel. In these ways, as N. Scott Momaday (1974) has observed, men and women learn to *appropriate* their landscapes, to think and act "with" them as well as about and upon them, and to weave them with spoken words into the very foundations of social life.[1] And in these ways, too, as every ethnographer eventually comes to appreciate, geographical landscapes are never culturally vacant. The ethnographic challenge is to fathom what it is that a particular landscape, filled to brimming with past and present significance, can be called upon to "say," and what, through the saying, it can be called upon to "do."

But where to begin and how to proceed? How, in any community, to identify the conceptual frameworks and verbal practices with which members appropriate their geography? One promising approach, as I have been suggesting, is to attend to native place-names and the full variety of communicative functions served by acts of naming in different social contexts. It may be noted in this regard that place-names, or toponyms, comprise a distinct semantic domain in the lexicons of all known languages, and that the formal properties of place-name systems, together with their spatial correlates and etymological histories, have long been objects of anthropological inquiry. But the common activity of placenaming—the actual use of toponyms in concrete instances of everyday speech—has attracted little attention from linguists or ethnographers. Less often still has placenaming been investigated as a universal means—and, it could well turn out, a universally primary means—for appropriating physical environments.

The reasons for this innocuous piece of scholarly neglect are several, but the main one arises from a widespread view of language in which proper names are assumed to have meaning solely in their capacity to refer and, as agents of reference, to enter into simple and complex predications. Many of the limitations imposed by this narrow conception of meaning have been exposed and criticized in recent years, most ably by linguistic anthropologists and philosophers of language who have shown that reference, though unquestionably a vital linguistic function, is but one of many that spoken utterances can be made to perform. But despite these salutary developments, and unhappily for students who seek to understand linguistic meaning as an emergent property of verbal interaction, the idea persists in many quarters that proper names, including toponyms, serve as referential vehicles whose only purpose is to denote, or "pick out," objects in the world.[2]

If a certain myopia attaches to this position, there is irony as well, for place-names are arguably among the most highly charged and richly evocative of all linguistic symbols. Because of their inseparable connection to specific localities, place-names may be used to summon forth an enormous range of mental and emotional associations—associations of time and space, of history and events, of persons and social activities, of oneself and stages in one's life. And in their capacity to evoke, in their compact power to muster and consolidate so much of what a landscape may be taken to represent in both personal and cultural terms, place-names acquire a functional value that easily matches their utility as instruments of reference. Most notably, as T. S. Eliot (1932) and Seamus Heaney (1980) have remarked, place-names provide materials for resonating ellipses, for speaking and writing in potent shorthand, for communicating much while saying very little. Poets and songwriters have long understood that economy of expression may enhance the quality and force of aesthetic discourse, and that place-names stand ready to be exploited for this purpose. Linguists and anthropologists would do well to understand that in many communities, similar considerations may influence common forms of spoken interaction, and that in this arena too, place-names may occupy a privileged position. For these and other reasons, an ethnographic approach to the activity of placenaming seems well worth pursuing. The present chapter, which now takes a sharp ethnographic turn, is offered as an illustration of where such an approach may lead, and why, beyond the illumination of specific cases, it may also shed light on matters of general interest.

Speaking with Names

The Western Apache residents of Cibecue are not averse to talking about each other, and some of them—like Lola Machuse—seem to enjoy it immensely. "I'm intress in evybody!" Lola will exclaim in her distinctive variety of English, and everyone in Cibecue knows she speaks the truth. Just over sixty, she is a handsome woman with large brown eyes, a sharply defined nose, and splendidly shaped hands that are hardly ever still. The mother of eight children, she divides her time between caring for the needs of her family, collecting plants for use in herbal medicines, participating in ceremonial activities, and farming. She also keeps fully informed on what happens in her village and, like other Apache women who have led exemplary lives, is frequently invited to comment on current events. And comment on them she does—intelligently, insightfully, usually sympathetically, and with a lively enthusiasm for nuance and detail that is sometimes as amusing as it is mildly overwhelming. Western Apache communities, like small communities everywhere, operate largely by word of mouth, and people from Cibecue have suggested more than once that Lola Machuse is practically a community unto herself. Unfailingly cheerful and completely at ease with herself, she is a compassionate person with a spirited zest for life.

It is a hot afternoon in the middle of July and Lola Machuse is working at home. Seated in the shade of a large brush-covered ramada, she is mending clothes in the company of her husband, Robert, two Apache women named Emily and Louise, and another visitor, myself, who has come to settle a small debt and get a drink of water.[3] The heat of the afternoon is heavy and oppressive, and there is little to do but gaze at the landscape that stretches out before us: a narrow valley, bisected by a stream lined with stately cottonwood trees, which rises abruptly to embrace a broken series of red sandstone bluffs, and, beyond the bluffs, a flat expanse of grassy plain ending in the distance at the base of a low range of mountains. Fearsome in the blazing sun, the country around Cibecue lies motionless and inert, thinly shrouded in patches of bluish haze. Nothing stirs except for Clifford, the Machuses' ancient yellow dog, who shifts his position in the dust, groans fitfully, and snaps at a fly. Silence.

The silence is broken by Louise, who reaches into her oversized purse for a can of Pepsi-Cola, jerks it open with a loud snap, and begins to speak in the Cibecue dialect of Western Apache. She speaks softly, haltingly, and with long pauses to accentuate the seriousness of what she is saying. Late last night, she reports, sickness assailed her younger brother. Painful cramps gnawed at his stomach. Numbness crept up his legs and into his thighs. He vomited three times in rapid succession. He looked extremely pale. In the morning, just before dawn, he was driven to the hospital at Whiteriver. The people who had gathered at his home were worried and frightened and talked about what happened. One of them, Louise's cousin, recalled that several months ago, when the young man was working on a cattle roundup near a place named Tsį Biyi'itiné (Trail Extends Into A Grove Of Sticklike Trees), he had inadvertently stepped on a snakeskin that lay wedged in a crevice between some rocks. Another member of the roundup crew, who witnessed the incident, cautioned the young man that contact with snakes is always dangerous and urged him to immediately seek the services of a 'snake medicine person' (*tł'iish bi diiyin*). But Louise's younger brother had only smiled, remarking tersely that he was not alarmed and that no harm would befall him.

Louise, who is plainly worried and upset by these events, pauses and sips from her drink. After a minute or so, having regained her composure, she begins to speak again. But Lola Machuse quietly interrupts her. Emily and Robert will speak as well. What follows is a record of their discourse, together with English translations of the utterances.[4]

> Louise: Shidizhé . . . (My younger brother . . .)
> Lola: Tséé Hadigaiyé yú 'ágodzaa. (It happened at Line Of White Rocks Extends Up And Out, at this very place!)
> [Pause: 30–45 seconds]
> Emily: Ha'aa. Túzhį' Yaahigaiyé yú 'ágodzaa. (Yes. It happened at Whiteness Spreads Out Descending To Water, at this very place!)
> [Pause: 30–45 seconds]
> Lola: Da'aníí. K'is Deeschii' Naaditiné yú 'ágodzaa. (Truly. It happened at Trail Extends Across A Red Ridge With Alder Trees, at this very place!)
> Louise: [laughs softly]
> Robert: Gozhǫǫ doleeł. (Pleasantness and goodness will be forthcoming.)
> Lola: Gozhǫǫ doleeł. (Pleasantness and goodness will be forthcoming.)
> Louise: Shidizhé bíni'éshid ne góshé? (My younger brother is foolish, isn't he, dog?)

Following this brief exchange, talk ceases under the brush-covered ramada and everyone retreats into the privacy of his or her thoughts. Louise drinks again from her can of Pepsi-Cola and passes it on to Emily. Lola Machuse returns to her sewing, while Robert studies a horse in a nearby corral. Only Clifford, who has launched a feverish attack on an itch below his ear, seems unaffected by what has been said. Silence once again.

But what *has* been said? To what set of personal and social ends? And why in such a clipped and cryptic fashion? If these questions create problems for us (and I think it can be assumed that they do), it is because we are dealing with a spate of conversation whose organization eludes us, a strip of Western Apache verbal doings whose animating aims and purposes seem obscure. But why? The problem is not that the literal meanings of utterances comprising the conversation are difficult to grasp. On the contrary, anyone with a passing knowledge of Western Apache grammar could attest that each of the utterances is well-formed in all respects and that each presents one or more simple claims whose positive truth-value no Apache would presume to dispute. It is not, then, on the surface of the utterances—or, as linguists prefer to say, at the level of their propositional content—that our interpretive difficulties lie.

What is puzzling about this snippet of Western Apache talk is that we are unable to account for the ways in which its constituent utterances are related to each other. Put more exactly, we lack the knowledge required to establish sequential relations among the utterances, the unstated premises and assumptions that order the utterances, just as they occur, into a piece of meaningful discourse. It is by no means evident, for example, how Lola Machuse's statement ("It happened at Line Of White Rocks Extends Up And Out, at this very place!") should be related to Louise's narrative about her ailing brother. Neither is it clear how Emily's assertion ("Yes. It happened at Whiteness Spreads Out Descending To Water, at this very place!") should be interpreted as a response to the narrative or to Lola's prior statement. What are we to make of Lola's response to Emily ("Truly. It happened at Trail Extends Across A Red Ridge With Alder Trees, at this very place!")? And why should it be, as things are coming to a close, that Louise sees fit to address the Machuses' dog? Our puzzlement persists throughout, causing us to experience the text of the conversation as fragmented and disjointed, as oddly unmotivated, as failing to come together as a whole. In short, we are unable to place a construction on the text that invests it with *coherence,* and so, in the end, we cannot know what the conversation itself may have been about. Lola Machuse and her companions have surely accomplished something with their talk. But what?

The episode at the Machuses' home exemplifies a venerable practice with which Western Apache speakers exploit the evocative power of place-names to comment on the moral conduct of persons who are absent from the scene. Called "speaking with names" (*yałti' bee'ízhí*), this verbal routine also allows those who engage in it to register claims about their own moral worth, about aspects of their social relationships with other people on hand, and about a particular way of attending to the local landscape that is avowed to produce a beneficial form of heightened self-awareness. And as if this were not enough, much of what gets said and done is attributed to unseen Apache ancestors who are prompted by the voices of conversational participants to communicate in a collective voice that no one actually hears. All in all, the practice of "speaking with names" is a subtle and subterranean affair.

To gain an understanding of this practice and the sources of its coherence for Western Apache people, I shall assume that spoken discourse is a cooperative activity in which individuals seek to accomplish a range of communicative purposes. I shall also assume that participants in many kinds of discourse use language to explore with each other the significance of past and potential events, drawing from these examinations certain consequences for their present and future actions. Finally, I shall assume that speakers pursue such objectives by producing utterances that are intended to perform several speech acts simultaneously, and that hearers, making dexterous use of relevant bodies of cultural knowledge, react and respond to these acts at different levels of abstraction. Spoken discourse, then, is more than a chain of situated utterances. Rather, as William Labov and David Fanshel (1977:26–28) have shown, discourse consists in a developing matrix of utterances and actions, bound together by a web of shared understandings pertinent to both, which serves as an expanding context for interpreting the meanings of utterances and actions alike. More a matter of linguistic function than of linguistic form, coherence in discourse is achieved when participants put their utterances to interlocking forms of mutually recognizable work. More a matter of implicit doings than of explicit sayings, coherence is what participants hear (though generally they fail to notice hearing it) when their work is going well.

In Lola Machuse's somnolent yard, where the work of discourse went off without a hitch, coherence was never in question. Neither was the smooth implementation of a Western Apache technique for appropriating the natural landscape, a distinctive cultural framework for interpreting the landscape and turning it by means of speech to

specific social ends. Never in question, that is, to anyone but myself—
a superfluous, slightly stupefied, and roundly perplexed outsider. What
did Lola Machuse and those other Apaches imagine themselves to be
up to as they sat around swapping place-names? How were they making sense, and what sort of sense were they making? What manner of
thinking informed their utterances and the actions their utterances
performed? What, in short, was the culture of their discourse?

"We Gave That Woman Pictures"

If the discourse at Lola Machuse's home is to be usefully understood, steps must be taken to enter the conceptual world of the people
who produced it. Needless to say, we cannot recover their experience
of their discourse as it actually occurred, what Maurice Merleau-Ponty
(1969:89) called the "inner experience of language-spoken-now." But
we can explore, retrospectively and therefore in reconstructive terms,
what participants in the encounter took their discourse to be about,
why they saw fit to contribute to it as they did, and how they interpreted the utterances and actions that composed it. In addition, we
can explore the culturally based assumptions and beliefs that made these
interpretations possible, the "linguistic ideology" with which persons
from Cibecue rationalize for themselves and explain to others what
spoken words are capable of doing when used in certain ways.[5] In
short, we can construct an ethnographic account of the speech event
itself, an interpretation of Apache interpretations that relates the event
to the body of thought that made its occurrence meaningful and to the
particular social circumstances that made its meaning unique.

All such undertakings profit from the guidance of experienced native instructors, and no one living at Cibecue is more capable or willing in this regard than Lola Machuse herself. So let us begin, as in fact
I did shortly after the episode at her camp took place, by considering
her account of what transpired as the women drank their Pepsi and
Clifford snapped at flies.

> We gave that woman [Louise] pictures to work on in her
> mind. We didn't speak too much to her. We didn't hold her
> down. That way she could travel in her mind. She could add
> on to them [the pictures] easily. We gave her clear pictures

with place-names. So her mind went to those places, standing in front of them as our ancestors did long ago. That way she could see what happened there long ago. She could hear stories in her mind, perhaps hear our ancestors speaking. She could recall the knowledge of our ancestors.

We call it speaking with names. Place-names are all we need for that, speaking with names. We just fix them up. That woman was too sad. She was worried too much about her younger brother. So we tried to make her feel better. We tried to make her think good thoughts. That woman's younger brother acted stupidly. He was stupid and careless. He failed to show respect. No good! We said nothing critical about him to her. We talked around it. Those place-names are strong! After a while, I gave her a funny story. She didn't get mad. She was feeling better. She laughed. Then she had enough, I guess. She spoke to the dog about her younger brother, criticizing him, so we knew we had helped her out.

Lola Machuse recorded this statement two days after the speech event at her home took place, and four days later, having discussed her account with all parties involved, I determined to treat it as a guide for subsequent inquiries. Everyone to whom I presented Lola's account agreed that it was encompassing and astute; it touched, they said, on everything that was essential for getting a proper sense of what "speaking with names" might be used to accomplish. But they also agreed that it was rather too highly condensed, a bare bones sort of interpretation, adequate for persons familiar with the practice but understandably opaque to a neophyte such as myself, and that it could profit from explication and fleshing out. Never one to be outdone, Lola Machuse agreed instantly with the agreers, saying she was well aware of the problem, thank you very much, and had understood all along that further instruction would be necessary. Sometimes talk is complicated, she observed, and one must move slowly to get to the bottom of it. So with all of us scrambling to agree with Lola, and with Lola herself firmly in charge, the fleshing out process began. Our work took longer than I had expected, but now, with much of it done, Lola Machuse's original account seems better to me than ever; it provides, as one of my older Apache consultants told me it would, a "straight path to knowing." And so I have used Lola's interpretation here, partitioned into convenient segments, as a model, a path of a different kind, for organizing and presenting my own.

> We gave that woman pictures to work on in her mind. We didn't speak too much to her. We didn't hold her down. That way she could travel in her mind. She could add on to them easily.

Western Apache conceptions of language and thought are cast in pervasively visual terms. Every occasion of 'speaking' (*yałti'*) provides tangible evidence of 'thinking' (*natsíkees*), and thinking occurs in the form of 'pictures' (*be'elzaahí*) that persons 'see' (*yo'įį*) in their minds. Prompted by a desire to 'display thinking' (*nil'įį natsíkees*), speaking involves the use of language to 'depict' (*'e'ele'*) and 'convey' (*yo'áál*) these images to the members of an audience, such that they, on 'hearing' (*yidits'ag*) and 'holding' (*yotą'*) the speaker's words, can 'view' (*yínel'įį*) the images in their own minds. Thinking, as Apaches conceive of it, consists in picturing to oneself and attending privately to the pictures. Speaking consists in depicting one's pictures for other people, who are thus invited to picture these depictions and respond to them with depictions of their own. Discourse, or 'conversation' (*'iłch'į' yádaach'ilti'*), consists in a running exchange of depicted pictures and pictured depictions, a reciprocal representation and visualization of the ongoing thoughts of participating speakers.

But things are not really so neat and tidy. According to consultants from Cibecue, the depictions offered by Western Apache speakers are invariably incomplete. Even the most gifted and proficient speakers contrive to leave things out, and small children, who have not yet learned to indulge in such contrivances, leave out many things. Consequently, Apache hearers must always 'add on' (*'ínágodn'aah*) to depictions made available to them in conversation, augmenting and supplementing these spoken images with images they fashion for themselves. This process is commonly likened to adding stones to a partially finished wall, or laying bricks upon the foundation of a house, because it is understood to involve a 'piling up' (*łik'iyitł'ih*) of new materials onto like materials already in place. It is also said to resemble the rounding up of livestock: the 'bringing together' (*dalaházhį'ch'indíí*) of cattle or horses from scattered locations to a central place where other animals have been previously gathered. These metaphors all point to the same general idea, which is that depictions provided by Apache speakers are treated by Apache hearers as bases on which to build, as projects to complete, as invitations to exercise the imagination.

Western Apaches regard spoken conversation as a form of 'voluntary cooperation' (*łich'į' 'odaach'idii*) in which all participants are entitled to displays of 'respect' (*yińłsįh*). Accordingly, whenever people speak in cordial and affable tones, considerations of 'kindness and politeness' (*bił goch'oba'*) come centrally into play. Such considerations may influence Apache speech in a multitude of ways, but none is more basic than the courtesy speakers display by refraining from 'speaking too much' (*łąago yałti'*). Although the effects of this injunction are most clearly evident in the spare verbal style employed by Apache storytellers, people from Cibecue insist that all forms of narration benefit from its application. And the reasons, they explain, are simple enough.

A person who speaks too much—someone who describes too busily, who supplies too many details, who repeats and qualifies too many times—presumes without warrant on the right of hearers to build freely and creatively on the speaker's own depictions. With too many words, such a speaker acts to 'smother' (*biká' yinłkaad*) his or her audience by seeming to say, arrogantly and coercively, "I *demand* that you see everything that happened, how it happened, and why it happened, *exactly* as I do." In other words, persons who speak too much insult the imaginative capabilities of other people, "blocking their thinking," as one of my consultants said in English, and "holding down their minds." So Western Apache narrators consistently take a different tack, implying by the economical manner of their speech, "I will depict just enough for you to see what happened, how it happened, and perhaps why it happened. Add on to these depictions however you see fit." An effective narrator, people from Cibecue report, never speaks too much; an effective narrator takes steps to "open up thinking," thereby encouraging his or her listeners to "travel in their minds."[6]

Figure 5   *T'iis Bitł'áh Tú 'Olíné (Water Flows Inward Under A Cottonwood Tree).*

We gave her clear pictures with place-names. So her mind went
to those places, standing in front of them as our ancestors did long
ago. That way she could see what happened there long ago.
She could hear stories in her mind, perhaps hear our ancestors
speaking. She could recall the knowledge of our ancestors.

Nothing is more basic to the telling of a Western Apache story than
identifying the geographical locations at which events in the story
unfold. For unless Apache listeners are able to picture a physical setting for narrated events—unless, as one of my consultants said, "your
mind can travel to that place and really see it"—the events themselves
will be difficult to imagine. This is because events in the narrative will
seem to happen nowhere, and such an idea, Apaches assert, is prepos-
terous and disquieting. Placeless events are an impossibility; everything that happens must happen somewhere. The location of an event

Figure 6 Tséé Ligai Dah Sidilé (White Rocks Lie Above In A Compact Cluster).

is an integral aspect of the event itself, and identifying the event's location is therefore essential to properly depicting—and effectively picturing—the event's occurrence. For these reasons, placeless stories simply do not get told. Instead, all Apache narratives are verbally anchored to points upon the land with precise depictions of specific locations. And what these depictions are accomplished with—what the primary spatial anchors of Apache narratives almost always turn out to be—are place-names.[7]

Some appreciation of the descriptive precision of Western Apache place-names can be gained by matching names with photographs of their geographical referents. By way of illustration, consider the three names listed below, which have been segmented into their constituent morphemes and whose referents are shown in figures 5–7.

Figure 7 *Tséé Biká' Tú Yaahilíné (Water Flows Down On A Succession Of Flat Rocks).*

T'iis Bitł'áh Tú 'Olíné: *T'iis* (cottonwood tree) + *Bitł'áh* (under it; beneath it) + *Tú* (water) + *'O-* (inward) + *-lí-* (it flows) + *-né* (the one).
Translation: Water Flows Inward Under A Cottonwood Tree

Tséé Łigai Dah Sidilé: *Tséé* (rock; stone) + *Łigai* (white; whiteness) + *Dah* (above ground level) + *Sidil* (three or more form a compact cluster) + *-é* (the one).
Translation: White Rocks Lie Above In A Compact Cluster

Tséé Biká' Tú Yaahilíné: *Tséé* (rock; stone) + *Biká'* (on top of it; a flattish object) + *Tú* (water) + *Yaa-* (downward) + *-hi-* (linear succession of regularly repeated movements) + *-lí* (it flows) + *-né* (the one).
Translation: Water Flows Down On A Succession Of Flat Rocks

88

As the photographs suggest, Western Apache place-names provide more than precise depictions of the sites to which the names refer. In addition, place-names implicitly identify positions for *viewing* these locations: optimal vantage points, so to speak, from which the sites can be observed, clearly and unmistakably, just as their names depict them. To picture a site from its name, then, requires that one imagine it as if standing or sitting at a particular spot, and it is to these privileged positions, Apaches say, that the images evoked by place-names cause them to travel in their minds.

Wherever the optimal vantage point for a named site may be located—east of the site or west, above it or below, near it or at some distance away—the vantage point is described as being 'in front of' (*bádnyú*) the site; and it is there, centuries ago, that ancestors of the Western Apache are believed to have stood when they gave the site its name. Accordingly, consultants from Cibecue explain that in positioning people's minds to look 'forward' (*bidááh*) into space, a place-name also positions their minds to look 'backward' (*t'ąązhi'*) into time. For as persons imagine themselves standing in front of a named site, they may imagine that they are standing in their 'ancestors' tracks' (*nohwizą'yé biké'é*), and from this psychological perspective, which is sometimes described as an intense form of 'daydreaming' (*bił 'onaagodah*), traditional accounts of ancestral events associated with the site are said to be recalled with singular clarity and force.

The capacity of Western Apache place-names to situate people's minds in historical time and space is clearly apparent when names are used to anchor traditional narratives that depict ancestral life and illustrate aspects of 'ancestral knowledge' (*nohwizą'yé bi kigoyą'íí*).[8] But the evocative power of place-names is most forcefully displayed when a name is used to substitute for the narrative it anchors, 'standing up alone' (*'o'áá*), as Apaches say, to symbolize the narrative as well as the knowledge it contains. On such occasions, a single place-name may accomplish the communicative work of an entire saga or historical tale, and sometimes, depending on the immediate social circumstances, it may accomplish even more. For when place-names are employed in this isolated and autonomous fashion—when, in other words, Apache people practice "speaking with names"—their actions are interpreted as a recommendation to recall ancestral stories and apply them directly to matters of pressing personal concern. And in emotionally charged contexts like these, my consultants maintain, 'ancestral voices' (*nohwizą'yé bizhíí*) may seem to speak directly to the individuals involved.[9]

> We call it speaking with names. Place-names are all we need
> for that, speaking with names. We just fix them up. That
> woman was too sad. She was worried too much about her
> younger brother. So we tried to make her feel better.
> We tried to make her think good thoughts.

Speaking with names is considered appropriate under certain conditions only, and these conditions tend to occur infrequently. Consequently, as people from Cibecue are quick to point out, place-names are usually put to other communicative ends. Most of the time, place-names are called upon to perform simple verbal chores: to indicate where one is going, for example, or to announce where one has been; to make plans for a forthcoming hunt, or to pinpoint the latest happenings gleaned from local gossip. When place-names are used for ordinary purposes such as these, Apache speakers typically produce the names in shortened or contracted forms. Thus, the name T'iis Bitłáh Tú 'Olį́į' (Water Flows Inward Under A Cottonwood Tree) is commonly heard as T'iis Tl'áh 'Olį́į' or T'iis Tú 'Olį́į', the name Tséé Biká' Tú Yaahilį́į' (Water Flows Down On A Succession Of Flat Rocks) as Tséé Ká' Yaahilį́į' or Tséé Tú Yahilį́į', and so forth. In marked contrast to these abbreviated renderings, place-names intended to evoke mental pictures of the past are invariably spoken in full and are embellished, or 'fixed up' (*náyidlé*), with an optional suffix that imparts an emphatic force roughly equivalent to English "right here!" or "at this very place!" Accordingly, the place-name T'iis Bitł'áh Tú 'Olį́į' is produced in traditional narratives as T'iis Bitł'áh Tú 'Olį́né, the name Tséé Biká' Tú Yaahilį́į' as Tséé Biká' Tú Yaahilį́né, and so forth. Although the optional suffix may be employed for purposes other than helping to summon ancestral images and voices, my consultants agree that this is one of its primary functions. And at no time is that function as readily apparent as when Apache men and women, bent upon speaking with names, dispense with narratives completely and use place-names in the expression X *'ágodzaa yú* (It happened at X, at this very place!).

This expression is normally reserved for social situations in which speaking of absent parties to persons closely connected to them must be accomplished with delicacy and tact. Specifically, the expression is used when ancestral knowledge seems applicable to difficulties arising from serious errors in someone else's judgment, but when voicing one's thoughts on the matter might be taken as evidence of arrogance, critical disapproval, or lack of sympathetic understanding. Instead, speaking with names enables those who engage in it to acknowledge a regrettable circumstance without explicitly judging it, to exhibit solicitude without openly proclaiming it, and to offer advice without appearing to do so.

But speaking with names accomplishes more than this. A traditional Apache narrative encapsulated in its own spatial anchor, the expression X *'ágodzaa yú* is also a call to memory and imagination. Simultaneously, it is a call to persons burdened by worry and despair to take remedial action on behalf of themselves. "Travel in your mind," the expression urges those to whom it is addressed. "Travel in your mind to a point from which to view the place whose name has just been spoken. Imagine standing there, as if in the tracks of your ancestors, and recall stories of events that occurred at that place long ago. Picture these events in your mind and appreciate, as if the ancestors were speaking to you directly, the knowledge the stories contain. Bring this knowledge to bear on your own disturbing situation. Allow the past to inform your understanding of the present. You will feel better if you do."

And Western Apache people report that sometimes they do feel better. Having pictured distant places and dwelled on ancestral events, their worries become less acute: less 'sharp' (*ts'ik'ii*), less 'hard' (*ntł'iz*), less 'noisy' (*gońch'aad*) in their minds. Feelings of anxiety and emotional turbulence may give way to welcome sensations of 'smoothness' (*dilkǫǫh*), of 'softness' (*dédi'ilé*), of growing inner 'quiet' (*doohwaa gońch'aada*). And when this actually happens—when ancestral knowledge works to give beneficial perspective and fresh recognition that trying times can be dealt with successfully and eventually overcome—

persons thus heartened may announce that relationships characterized by 'pleasantness and goodness' (*gozhǫǫ*) have been restored between themselves and their surroundings. A psychological balance has been reestablished, an optimistic outlook born of strengthened confidence and rejuvenated hope, and people may also announce that a 'sickness' (*nezgai*) has been 'healed' (*nábilziih*). 'Bad thinking' (*nchǫ'go natsíkęęs*) has been replaced by 'good thinking' (*nzhǫǫgo natsíkęęs*), and at least for a while the exigencies of life can be met with replenished equanimity.

"Those Place-names Are Strong"

The foregoing account of aspects of Western Apache place-name ideology supplies the basic conceptual framework with which to interpret the conversational encounter at the Machuses' home in Cibecue. But because the account has been formulated as Apache people themselves insist upon doing—that is, in abstract normative terms—it fails to elucidate what the practice of speaking with names served to accomplish on that particular occasion. In other words, we have yet to identify the social actions that participants in the encounter used their utterances to perform, and thus, necessarily, we have yet to grasp the coherence of their talk. So let us be about it. Having fashioned an account of the cultural logic on which speaking with names is understood to operate, attention may now be directed to an interpretation of how, and with what sorts of interpersonal consequences, this conversational practice was actually put to work. Once again, Lola Machuse.

> That woman's younger brother acted stupidly. He was stupid
> and careless. He failed to show respect. No good! We said
> nothing critical about him to her. We talked around it.

The social gathering at Lola Machuse's ramada was uncomfortable for everyone, but especially for Louise. Troubled by her brother's sudden illness, she was troubled even more by his apparent lack of common sense. Having come into contact with the snakeskin near the roundup camp, he should have gone directly to a ritual specialist for assistance in dealing with his contaminated state. That he failed to do so was disturbing enough, but that he treated the incident in such cavalier fashion was more disturbing still. Plainly, he was guilty of a grave lapse in judgment, and now, as surely he could have anticipated, he was suffering the painful consequences. Why had the young man acted so irresponsibly? In addition to being upset, Louise was sorely perplexed.

Louise's chronicle of her brother's misfortune created an opportunity for all on hand to comment on his conduct. But because her account portrayed him in a distinctly unfavorable light, it also presented him as a target for easy criticism. If criticism were to be forthcoming, it could only serve to embarrass Louise, for she would have no alternative but to try to defend her brother's actions—and this would be awkward and difficult at best. Yet refusing to defend him could be taken to mean that she was prepared to condemn him entirely, and condemning one's relatives, especially in the presence of nonrelatives, is a conspicuous violation of kinship loyalties that Western Apaches rarely see fit to excuse.[10]

For these reasons, Louise's candid statement placed her companions in a delicate dilemma. On the one hand, no one could assert that Louise's brother had not acted wrongly without casting serious doubt on his or her own good judgment. On the other hand, no one could openly censure the young man without adding to Louise's discomfort, thereby displaying a lack of consideration for her feelings and a lack of concern for the circumstances that had produced them. How, then, to respond? How to speak the truth—or something that could be heard as not denying the truth—without exacerbating an already sensitive situation?

> Those place-names really helped us out! We gave her pictures with place-names. That way she started feeling better. Those place-names are strong!

After finishing her account, Louise paused, took a long drink of Pepsi-Cola, and started to speak again of her beleaguered brother. But Lola Machuse intervened at this point, saying softly but firmly, "Tséé Hadigaiyé yú 'ágodzaa" (It happened at Line Of White Rocks Extends Up And Out, at this very place!). Lola's utterance was intended to evoke a historical tale for Louise to picture in her mind, but it was also designed to change the topic of talk and set the conversation on a new and different course. Instead of Louise's brother, whom Lola was showing she had no desire to criticize, attention was shifted to Louise herself and her troubled reactions to her brother's predicament. Instead of disapproval, Lola Machuse was exhibiting sympathy and concern.

As later told by herself, the historical tale that Lola Machuse wished to evoke for Louise was the following.

It happened at Line Of White Rocks Extends Up And Out.
Long ago, a girl lived alone with her maternal grandmother.
Her grandmother sent her out regularly to collect firewood.
She went to a place above her camp. She could get there quickly
by climbing up through a rocky canyon. Many snakes lived there.
So her grandmother told her always to go another way.
Then the girl went to collect firewood. The day was hot.
Then the girl became thirsty. Then she thought, "This wood
is heavy. I don't want to carry it too far." Then she started to
walk down the rocky canyon. There were loose rocks where
she walked. Then she slipped and fell down. The firewood
she was carrying scattered everywhere! Then she started to
pick it up. A snake bit her hand! Then she got scared.
"My grandmother knew this would happen to me," she thought.
Then the girl returned to where she was living with her
grandmother. Her arm and hand became badly swollen.
Then they worked over her [performed a curing ceremony].
Later, the girl went to her grandmother. "My life is still my
own," she said. Then her grandmother talked to her again.
Now she knew how to live right.
It happened at Line Of White Rocks Extends Up And Out.

As Lola Machuse had reason to suspect, Louise knew this story well. She had heard it many times and on several occasions had performed it for her own children. Consequently, Louise reported later, her mind traveled instantly to a spot from which to view Line Of White Rocks Extends Up And Out, and images of the girl who was bitten by the snake appeared just as quickly. As a lengthy silence descended on the Machuse camp at Cibecue, Louise's thoughts moved along these lines.

A bad thing happened at that place. Very bad! I saw that girl.
She was impulsive. She forgot to be careful. She ceased

showing respect. She was like my younger brother. She ceased thinking properly, so something bad happened to her. She became very scared but recovered from it. She almost died but held onto her own life.

Lola Machuse's evocative comment had a calming effect on everyone sitting beneath the ramada at her home. Her statement relieved Louise of any need to publicly defend her brother's conduct and, at the same time, charted a conversational path that others could easily follow. Acknowledging the felicity of that path, and taking steps to pursue it, Emily produced a similar statement of her own—"Ha'aa. Túzhį' Yaahigaiyé yú 'ágodzaa." (Yes. It happened at Whiteness Spreads Out Descending To Water, at this very place!)—and once again Louise was urged to travel in her mind and picture a historical tale.

Emily's version of this tale, which she said has been slightly abridged, is as follows.

It happened at Whiteness Spreads Out Descending To Water.
Long ago, a boy went to hunt deer. He rode on horseback. Pretty soon he saw one [a deer], standing on the side of a canyon. Then he went closer and shot it. He killed it. Then the deer rolled all the way down to the bottom of the canyon.

Then the boy went down there. It was a buck, fat and muscular. Then he butchered it. The meat was heavy, so he had to carry it up in pieces. He had a hard time reaching the top of the canyon with each piece.

Now it was getting dark. One hindquarter was still lying at the bottom of the canyon. "I have enough meat already," he thought. So he left the hindquarter where it was lying. He left it there.

Then he packed his horse and started to ride home. Then the boy got dizzy and nearly fell off his horse. Then his nose twitched uncontrollably, like Deer's nose does. Then pain shot up behind his eyes. Then he became scared.

Now he went back to the canyon. It was dark when he got there. He walked down to where the hindquarter was lying— but it was gone! Then he returned to his horse. He rode fast to where he was living with his relatives.

The boy was sick for a long time. The people prayed
for him on four separate occasions. He got better slowly.

No deer would present themselves to him. He said to his
children: "Look at me now. I failed to be careful when I was a
boy and now I have a hard time getting meat for you to eat."

It happened at Whiteness Spreads Out Descending To Water.

The actions performed by Emily's utterance were readily apparent
to Louise. Emily, like Lola Machuse before her, was attempting to
distract Louise with constructive thoughts and comfort her with expressions of support. But Louise was not intimately familiar with the
story of the boy and the deer, and though her mind went swiftly to a
point near Whiteness Spreads Out Descending To Water, she had
difficulty picturing all the events in the story. She did, however, have
one vivid image—of the pain-ridden boy struggling to stay astride his
horse—and this was sufficient to remind her of her brother. In addition, Louise said later, she could hear the boy, now an adult, as he
spoke to his children about his fateful mistake.

It was like I could hear some old man talking. He was talking
to his children. "I was impatient, so I left behind good meat
from that deer. Then I became very sick and very scared. I
failed to show respect." Even so, that boy lived on and grew
up and had children. He learned to think right, so he talked to
his children about it. Maybe my brother will learn to improve
his thinking like that.

The historical tale evoked by Emily is similar in several respects to
the tale evoked by Lola Machuse, and at this point in the proceedings,
Louise probably sensed that a pattern was starting to form. In both of
the stories, young people are depicted as irresponsible and disrespectful,
but for reasons having solely to do with their innocence and naivete.
In both stories, they suffer life-threatening consequences—serious illness and intense fright—from which they learn to avoid carelessness
and impatience in the future. Finally, and most important of all, they
regain their health and continue living, presumably for many years.
Thus the unstated message for Louise, which is also a prominent aspect of Western Apache ancestral knowledge, was a positive one: in

effect, "Take heart. These things happen. Young people make foolish and dangerous mistakes, but they usually profit from them and the
mistakes are seldom fatal. Be optimistic. There is reason to believe
your brother will recover."

> After a while, I gave her a funny story. She didn't get mad. She
> was feeling better. She laughed. Then she had enough, I
> guess. She spoke to the dog about her younger brother,
> criticizing him, so we knew we had helped her out.

Following another lengthy silence inside the brush ramada, Lola
Machuse acted to affirm and consolidate the tacit messages communicated thus far with a place-name intended to evoke a third historical
tale with similarities to the previous two. But with this utterance—
"Da'aníí. K'is Deeschii' Naaditiné yú 'ágodzaa." (Truly. It happened
at Trail Extends Across A Red Ridge With Alder Trees, at this very
place!)—she took a moderate risk. Although it deals with serious
matters, the story Lola was thinking of presents a humorous aspect,
and one of her purposes in evoking it was to lighten Louise's spirits
(and everyone else's) by striking a note of reserved good cheer. The
risk Lola ran was that her action would be perceived as intemperate,
perhaps even playful, and thus inappropriate to the seriousness and
solemnity of Louise's troubled circumstances.

This is the historical tale, as narrated by herself, that Lola Machuse
had in mind.

> It happened at Trail Extends Across A Red Ridge With
> Alder Trees.
> A boy and a girl were newly married. He didn't know that
> he should stay away from her when her grandmother came to
> visit [when she was having her menstrual period]. Then he
> tried to bother her. "Don't! I'm no good for that," she said.
> He was impatient. Then he tried to bother her again.
> Then she gave in.
> Then the boy got sick, they say. It was hard for him to sit
> down. Then his penis became badly swollen. Pissing was
> painful for him, too. He walked around clutching his crotch.
> He was deeply embarrassed in front of his wife and her

relatives. Then he got scared. "I wonder if I will be this way forever," he thought.

Then someone talked to him, saying "Don't bother your wife when her grandmother comes to visit. Stay away from her." Then that person gave the boy some medicine, saying "Drink this. It will make you well. Then you can stop being embarrassed. Then you can stop walking around clutching your crotch!" That is all.

It happened at Trail Extends Across A Red Ridge With Alder Trees.

Fortunately, Lola Machuse's lighthearted gamble did not misfire. Louise traveled in her mind to a vantage point from which to picture Trail Extends Across A Red Ridge With Alder Trees, viewed the crestfallen lad with his hand where it should never be seen in public, and returned from the journey mildly amused. Afterwards, Louise made these comments.

Everyone knows that story. My mind went there. It's funny to see that boy in the story holding onto himself. He should have left his wife alone. He was impulsive. He didn't think right. Then he got scared. Then he was made well again with medicine. . . . I've heard that story often, but it's always funny to see that boy holding onto himself, so shy and embarrassed.

At the Machuses' home in Cibecue, Louise expressed her amusement by laughing softly. This was an auspicious sign! Though surely worried still, Louise had been moved to levity, and everyone could tell that her spirits had briefly improved. Here was evidence that the unspoken messages conveyed by Lola Machuse and Emily—messages of sympathy, consolation, and encouragement—had been usefully received. Here was an indication that ancestral knowledge was providing Louise with a measure of comfort and hope. Seizing the moment, Robert Machuse acted to make elements of these messages explicit, compressing their dominant thrust into one succinct statement. "Gozhǫǫ doleeł" (Pleasantness and goodness will be forthcoming), said Robert with quiet conviction. And moments later, endorsing his sentiments and adding conviction of her own, Lola Machuse repeated the same phrase: "Gozhǫǫ doleeł."

Touched by this display of friendly goodwill, and aware that some sort of acknowledgment of it was now in order, Louise responded by taking a deft and self-effacing step. In the form of a mock question addressed to Clifford, the Machuses' dog, she gently criticized her own brother: "Shidizhé bíni'éshid ne góshé?" (My younger brother is foolish, isn't he, dog?). This utterance accomplished several actions at once. First, by drawing attention away from herself, Louise gave notice that further evocations of traditional narratives could be politely dispensed with; in effect, "You have all done enough." Also, by directing her question to one who could not answer it, Louise indicated that additional discussion of her brother and his difficulties would serve no useful purpose; in effect, "Let the matter rest. There is nothing more to say." Finally, and most adroitly of all, by voicing the thought that had been on everyone's mind from the beginning—that Louise's brother had indeed acted foolishly—she contrived to thank them for their tact in not having voiced it; in effect, "This is the discrediting truth about my relative. I know it and I know that you know it. You were polite and thoughtful to refrain from expressing it."

As could have been predicted, Clifford did not respond to Louise's bogus query. Neither did anyone else. The speech event was over. A few minutes later, Louise and Emily rose to their feet, complained to each other about a sudden plentitude of flies, and set off together in search of a cold can of Pepsi-Cola. Lola Machuse resumed her sewing and Robert Machuse went to water his horse. The day was beginning to cool, and the landscape beyond Cibecue, its rugged contours softened now by patches of lengthening shadow, looked more hospitable than before.

Language, Landscape, and the Moral Imagination

The possibilities of human language are variously conceived and variously understood. Every culture, whether literate or not, includes beliefs about how language works and what it is capable of doing. Similarly, every culture contains beliefs about the kinds of social contexts in which these capabilities may be realized most effectively. That such beliefs are present in contemporary Western Apache culture should now be obvious, and that they may operate in telling ways to influence patterns of verbal interaction should likewise be apparent. Moreover, it should now be possible to appreciate how aspects of Western Apache linguistic ideology contribute to perceptions of coherence in one form of Apache discourse, and also why, when contextual conditions are right, that same ideology may invest the briefest of utterances with ample meaning and substantial expressive force.

The episode at Lola Machuse's home suggests that while coherence in Western Apache discourse can be usefully described as a product of interlocking utterances and actions, the expressive force of Apache discourse—what people from Cibecue call its 'strength' (*nalwod*)— may be viewed as a product of multiple interlockings at different levels of abstraction. Put more exactly, it is my impression that those utterances that perform the broadest range of mutually compatible actions at once are those that Apaches experience as having the greatest communicative impact. In other words, the expressive force of an Apache utterance seems to be roughly proportionate to the number of separate but complementary functions it accomplishes simultaneously, or, as Alton Becker (1982) has intimated, to the number of distinguishable subject matters it successfully communicates "about."

The Western Apache practice of "speaking with names" manifests just this sort of range and versatility. Thus, as we have seen, an utterance such as "Tséé Hadigaiyé yú 'ágodzaa" (It happened at Line Of White Rocks Extends Up And Out, at this very place!) may be used to accomplish all of the following actions: (1) produce a mental image of a particular geographical location; (2) evoke prior texts, such as historical tales and sagas; (3) affirm the value and validity of traditional moral precepts (i.e., ancestral knowledge); (4) display tactful and courteous attention to aspects of both positive and negative face; (5) convey sentiments of charitable concern and personal support; (6) offer practical advice for dealing with disturbing personal circumstances (i.e., apply ancestral knowledge); (7) transform distressing thoughts caused by excessive worry into more agreeable ones marked by optimism and hopefulness; and (8) heal wounded spirits.

This is a substantial amount for any spoken utterance to be able to accomplish, and what provides for the capability—what the forceful activity of speaking with names always communicates most basically "about"—is the cultural importance of named locations within the Western Apache landscape. Named places have long been symbols of rich significance for the Apache people, and place-names afford Apache speakers a ready means for appropriating that significance and turning it with brisk efficiency to specialized social ends. By virtue of their role as spatial anchors in traditional Apache narratives, place-names can be made to represent the narratives themselves, summarizing them, as it were, and condensing into compact form their essential moral truths. As a result, narratives and truths alike can be swiftly "activated" and brought into focused awareness through the use of place-names alone. And so it happens, on these occasions when Apache people see fit to speak with place-names, that a vital part of their tribal heritage seems to speak to them as well. For on such occasions, as we have seen, participants may be moved and instructed by voices other than their own. In addition, persons to whom place-names are addressed may be affected by the voices of their ancestors, voices that communicate in compelling silence with an inherent weight described by Mikhail Bakhtin as the "authoritative word":

> The authoritative word demands that we acknowledge it, that
> we make it our own; it binds us, quite independent of any
> power it might have to persuade us internally; we encounter it
> with its authority already fused on it. The authoritative word is
> located in a distanced zone, organically connected with a past
> that is felt to be hierarchically higher. Its authority was already
> acknowledged in the past. It is a prior discourse. . . . It is given
> (it sounds) in lofty spheres, not those of familiar contact. Its
> language is a special (as it were, hieratic) language. (Bakhtin
> 1981:342)

When Western Apache place-names are called upon to serve as vehicles of ancestral authority, the knowledge thus imparted is not so loftily given as to inhibit its use in the mundane spheres of everyday life. On the contrary, as the episode at the Machuses' home illustrates clearly, such knowledge exists to be applied, to be thought about and acted upon, to be incorporated (the more so the better, Lola Machuse would have us understand) into the smallest corners of personal and social experience. And insofar as this kind of incorporation occurs—

insofar as places and place-names provide Apache people with symbolic reference points for the moral imagination and its practical bearing on the actualities of their lives—the landscape in which the people dwell can be said to dwell in them. For the constructions Apaches impose upon their landscape have been fashioned from the same cultural materials as constructions they impose upon themselves as members of society. Both give expression to the same set of values, standards, and ideals; both are manifestations of the same distinctive charter for being-in-the-world. Inhabitants *of* their landscape, the Western Apache are thus inhabited *by* it as well, and in the timeless depth of that abiding reciprocity, the people and their landscape are virtually as one.

This reciprocal relationship—a relationship in which individuals invest themselves in the landscape while incorporating its meanings into their own most fundamental experience—is the ultimate source of the rich sententious potential and functional versatility of Western Apache place-names. For when place-names are used in the manner exemplified by Lola Machuse and her friends, the landscape is appropriated in pointedly social terms and the authoritative word of Apache tribal tradition is brought squarely to bear on matters of social concern. Concomitantly, persons in distress are reminded of what they already know but may sometimes forget—that ancestral knowledge is a powerful ally in times of adversity, and that reflecting upon it, as generations of Apaches have learned, can produce expanded awareness, feelings of relief, and a fortified ability to cope. And because helping people to cope is regarded by Apaches as a gesture of compassion, the use of place-names for this purpose serves as well to communicate solicitude, reassurance, and personal solidarity. The primary reason that speaking with names can accomplish so much—the reason its expressive force is sometimes felt so strongly—is that it facilitates reverberating acts of kindness and caring. And the effects of kindness and caring, especially when spirits are in need of healing, can be very strong indeed.

As must now be apparent, the ethnographic account presented in this chapter has been shaped by a view of spoken communication which rests on the premise that languages consist in shared economies of grammatical resources with which language users act to get things done. The resources of a language, together with the varieties of action facilitated by their use, acquire meaning and force from the sociocultural contexts in which they are embedded, and therefore, as every linguist knows, the discourse of any speech community exhibits a fundamental character—a genius, a spirit, an underlying personality—that is very much its own. Over a period of years, I have become convinced that one of the distinctive characteristics of Western Apache discourse is a predilection for performing a maximum of socially relevant actions with a minimum of linguistic means. Accordingly, I have been drawn to investigate instances of talk, like the one involving Lola and Robert Machuse, in which a few spoken words are made to accomplish large amounts of communicative work.[11] For it is on just such occasions, I believe, that elements of Apache culture and society fuse most completely with elements of grammar and the situated aims of individuals, such that very short utterances, like polished crystals refracting light, can be seen to contain them all. On these occasions, the Western Apache language is exploited to something near its full expressive potential, and even Apaches themselves, struck momentarily by the power of their discourse, may come away impressed.

Such powerful moments may not be commonplace in Western Apache speech communities, but they are certainly common enough—and when they occur, as on that hot and dusty day at Cibecue, robust worlds of meaning come vibrantly alive. Conveying these worlds, capturing with words both the richness of their content and the fullness of their spirit, requires an exacting effort at linguistic and cultural translation that can never be wholly successful. The problem, of course, is that verbally mediated realities are so densely textured and incorrigibly dynamic, and that one's own locutions for representing them fail to do justice to the numerous subtleties involved. Unavoidably, delicate proportions are altered and disturbed, intricate momentums halted and betrayed, and however much one explicates there is always more (or so one is tempted to suppose) that might usefully be done. Despite these persisting uncertainties, however, enough can be learned and understood so that we, like the people of Cibecue, may come away from certain kinds of speech events instructed and impressed and sometimes deeply moved. Following its more accentuated moments, moments shaped by graciousness and the resonating echoes of a fully present past, the minimalist genius of Western Apache discourse leaves us silent in its wake—traveling in our minds, listening for the ancestors, and studying the landscape with a new and different eye. On the pictorial wings of place-names, imaginations soar.

Wisdom Sits in Places

To know who you are, you have to have a place to come from.
—*Carson McCullers,* The Heart Is a Lonely Hunter

In this unsettled age, when large portions of the earth's surface are being ravaged by industrialism . . . when on several continents indigenous peoples are being forcibly uprooted by wanton encroachments upon their homelands . . . when American Indian tribes are mounting major legal efforts to secure permanent protection for sacred sites now controlled by federal agencies . . . when philosophers and poets are asserting that attachments to geographical localities contribute fundamentally to the formation of personal and social identities . . . when new forms of "environmental awareness" are being more radically charted and urgently advocated than ever in the past—in these disordered times, when contrasting ways of living in the world are generating unprecedented attention on a worldwide scale, it is unfortunate that anthropologists seldom study what people make of places.[1]

Sensitive to the fact that human existence is irrevocably situated in time and space, and keenly aware that social life is everywhere accomplished through an exchange of symbolic forms, anthropologists might be expected to report routinely on the varieties of meaning conferred by men and women on features of their natural surroundings. Yet ethnographic inquiry into cultural constructions of geographical realities is at best weakly developed. Willing enough to investigate the material and organizational means by which whole communities fashion workable adaptations to the physical environment, ethnographers have been notably less inclined to examine the elaborate arrays of conceptual and expressive instruments—ideas, beliefs, stories, songs—with which community members produce and display coherent understandings of it. Consequently, little is known of the ways in which culturally diverse peoples are alive to the world around them, of how they comprehend it, of the different modes of awareness with which they take it in and, in the words of Edmund Husserl, "discover that it matters." Nor can much be said about the effects of such discoveries on the persons who make them, about why some localities matter more than others, about why viewing a favored site (or merely recalling aspects of its appearance) may loosen strong emotions and kindle thoughts of a richly caring kind. In short, anthropologists have paid scant attention to one of the most basic dimensions of human experience—that close companion of heart and mind, often subdued yet potentially overwhelming, that is known as *sense of place*. Missing from the discipline is a thematized concern with the ways in which citizens of the earth constitute their landscapes and take themselves to be connected to them. Missing is a desire to fathom the various and variable perspectives from which people *know* their landscapes, the self-invested viewpoints from which (to borrow Isak Dinesen's felicitous image) they embrace the countryside and find the embrace returned. Missing is an interest in how men and women dwell.[2]

As formulated by Martin Heidegger (1977), whose general lead I propose to follow here, the concept of *dwelling* assigns importance to the forms of consciousness with which individuals perceive and apprehend geographical space.[3] More precisely, dwelling is said to consist in the multiple "lived relationships" that people maintain with places, for it is solely by virtue of these relationships that space acquires meaning. (Thus, as Heidegger [1977:332] himself put it, "spaces receive their essential being from particular localities and not from 'space' itself.") As numerous as they are both singular and specific, and fully realizable across great distances, relationships with places are lived whenever a place becomes the object of awareness. In many instances, awareness of place is brief and unselfconscious, a fleeting moment (a flash of recognition, a trace of memory) that is swiftly replaced by awareness of something else. But now and again, and sometimes without apparent cause, awareness is seized—arrested—and the place on which it settles becomes an object of spontaneous reflection and resonating sentiment. It is at times such as these, when individuals step back from the flow of everyday experience and attend self-consciously to places—when, we may say, they pause to actively sense them—that their relationships to geographical space are most richly lived and surely felt. For it is on these occasions of focused thought and quickened emotion that places are encountered most directly, experienced most robustly, and, in Heidegger's view, most fully brought into being. Sensing places, men and women become sharply aware of the complex attachments that link them to features of the physical world. Sensing places, they dwell, as it were, on aspects of dwelling.

Persons thus involved may also dwell on aspects of themselves, on sides and corners of their own evolving identities. For the self-conscious experience of place is inevitably a product and expression of the self whose experience it is, and therefore, unavoidably, the nature of that experience (its intentional thrust, its substantive content, its affective tones and colorings) is shaped at every turn by the personal and social biographies of those who sustain it.[4] Hence, as numerous writers have noted, places possess a marked capacity for triggering acts of self-reflection, inspiring thoughts about who one presently is, or memories of who one used to be, or musings on who one might become. And that is not all. Place-based thoughts about the self lead commonly to thoughts of other things—other places, other people, other times, whole networks of associations that ramify unaccountably within the expanding spheres of awareness that they themselves engender. The experience of sensing places, then, is thus both thoroughly reciprocal and incorrigibly dynamic. As places animate the ideas and feelings of persons who attend to them, these same ideas and feelings animate the places on which attention has been bestowed, and the movements of this process—inward toward facets of the self, outward toward aspects of the external world, alternately both together—cannot be known in advance. When places are actively sensed, the physical landscape becomes wedded to the landscape of the mind, to the roving imagination, and where the latter may lead is anybody's guess.

This process of interanimation relates directly to the fact that familiar places are experienced as inherently meaningful, their significance and value being found to reside in (and, it may seem, to emanate from) the form and arrangement of their observable characteristics. A concise account of this phenomenon, couched in a broader discussion of how people interact with material things, appears in the philosophical writings of Jean-Paul Sartre (1965:87–91). Proceeding on the twin assumptions that "man can only mean what he knows," and that "things can reflect for individuals only their own knowledge of them," Sartre considers what happens when attention is directed toward physical objects.

> When knowledge and feeling are oriented toward something
> real, actually perceived, the thing, like a reflector, returns the
> light it has received from it. As a result of this continual inter-
> action, meaning is continually enriched at the same time as
> the object soaks up affective qualities. The object thus
> obtains its own particular depth and richness. The affective
> state follows the progress of attention, developing with each
> new discovery of meaning . . . with the result that its develop-
> ment is unpredictable. At each moment perception overflows
> it and sustains it, and its density and depth come from its
> being confused with the perceived object. *Each quality is so
> deeply incorporated in the object that it is impossible to distinguish
> what is felt and what is perceived.* (Sartre 1965:89; emphasis
> added)

Thus, through a vigorous conflation of attentive subject and geographical object, places come to generate their own fields of meaning.[5] So, too, they give rise to their own aesthetic immediacies, their shifting moods and relevancies, their character and spirit. So, even in total stillness, places may seem to speak. But as Sartre makes clear, such voices as places possess should not be mistaken for their own. Animated by the thoughts and feelings of persons who attend to them, places express only what their animators enable them to say; like the thirsty sponges to which the philosopher alludes, they yield to consciousness only what consciousness has given them to absorb. Yet this may be quite considerable, and so it is, as everyone knows, that places actively sensed amount to substantially more than points in physical space. As natural "reflectors" that return awareness to the source from which it springs, places also provide points from which to look out on life, to grasp one's position in the order of things, to contemplate events from somewhere in particular. Human constructions par excellence, places consist in what gets made of them—in anything and everything they are taken to be—and their disembodied voices, immanent though inaudible, are merely those of people speaking silently to themselves.

And on numerous occasions, audibly enough, their voices are those of people speaking to each other. Although the self-conscious experience of place may at base be a private affair, tangible representations of it are commonly made available for public consumption. Indeed, as any seasoned traveler can readily attest, locally significant places get depicted and appraised by established local citizens almost as often as marital upheavals, bad weather, and the regrettable shortcomings of other people's children. Surrounded by places, and always in one place or another, men and women talk about them constantly, and it is from listening in on such exchanges and then trying to ascertain what has gotten said that interested outsiders can begin to appreciate what the encompassing landscape is really all about. Stated more exactly, the outsider must attempt to come to grips with the indigenous cultural forms that the landscape is experienced *with,* the shared symbolic vehicles that give shape to geographical experience and facilitate its communication—its re-creation and re-presentation—in interpersonal settings. For it is simply not the case, as some phenomenologists and growing numbers of nature writers would have us believe, that relationships to places are lived exclusively or predominantly in contemplative moments of social isolation. On the contrary, relationships to places are lived most often in the company of other people, and it is on these communal occasions—when places are sensed *together*—that native views of the physical world become accessible to strangers. And while attending to ordinary talk is always a useful strategy for uncovering such views, it is usually just a beginning. Relationships to places may also find expression through the agencies of myth, prayer, music, dance, art, architecture, and, in many communities, recurrent forms of religious and political ritual. Thus represented and enacted—

daily, monthly, seasonally, annually—places and their meanings are continually woven into the fabric of social life, anchoring it to features of the landscape and blanketing it with layers of significance that few can fail to appreciate. Deliberately and otherwise, people are forever presenting each other with culturally mediated images of where and how they dwell. In large ways and small, they are forever performing acts that reproduce and express their own sense of place—and also, inextricably, their own understandings of who and what they are.

As I conceive of it, the ethnographer's task is to determine what these acts of expression purportedly involve (why they are performed, how they are accomplished, what they are intended to achieve) and to disclose their importance by relating them to larger ideas about the world and its inhabitants. In other words, naturally occurring depictions of places are treated as actualizations of the knowledge that informs them, as outward manifestations of underlying systems of thought, as native constructions wrought with native materials that embody and display a native cast of mind. And it is that cast of mind (or certain prominent aspects of it, anyway) that the ethnographer must work to grasp, intelligibly make out, and later set down in writing. Heaven, then, in a few grains of carefully inspected sand; instructive statements about places and their role in human affairs through the close contextualization of a handful of telling events.[6]

An assignment of this delicacy challenges the text-building pen as much as it does the truth-seeking mind. Mulling over imperfect field notes, sorting through conflicting intuitions, and beset by a host of unanswered questions, the ethnographer must somehow fashion a written account that adequately conveys his or her understanding of other peoples' understandings. As must now be apparent, my own preference is for chronological narratives that move from interpretations of experience raw to those of experience digested, from moments of anxious puzzlement ("What the devil is going on here?") to subsequent ones of cautious insight ("I think perhaps I see."). Because that, more often than not, is how ethnographic fieldwork actually unfolds. It is a discomfiting business in which loose ends abound and little is ever certain. But with ample time, a dollop of patience, and steady guidance from interested native instructors, one does make measurable progress. To argue otherwise (and there is a bit of that around these days) is to dismiss ethnography as a valid source of cultural knowledge and turn it into a solipsistic sideshow, an ominous prospect only slightly less appealing than the self-engrossed meanderings of those who seek to promote it. As Isaiah Berlin remarked somewhere, it is better to write of things one believes one knows something about than to anguish in high despair over the manifold difficulties of knowing things at all. And better as well, having taken the plunge, to allow oneself to enjoy it. Doing ethnography can be a great deal of fun, and disguising the fact on paper, as though it were something to be ashamed of, is less than totally honest. It may also be less than effective. Current fashions notwithstanding, clenched teeth and furrowed brow are no guarantee of literary success. In crafting one's prose, as in going about one's fieldwork, it is always permissible—and sometimes highly informative—to smile and even to laugh.

It is permissible, too, to be pleased—and sometimes downright impressed—with things one happens to learn. From time to time, when luck is on their side, ethnographers stumble onto culturally given ideas whose striking novelty and evident scope seem to cry out for thoughtful consideration beyond their accustomed boundaries. Making these ideas available in perusable form is a worthy endeavor on general principles, but where places are concerned it is apt to prove especially illuminating. For where places are involved, attendant modes of dwelling are never far behind, and in this dimly lit region of the anthropological world—call it, if you like, the ethnography of lived topographies—much remains to be learned. Places and their sensings deserve our close attention. To continue to neglect them would be foolish and shortsighted. Intriguing discoveries await us, and the need to consider them thoughtfully grows stronger every day.

"The Trail of Wisdom"

June 7, 1982. The foregoing thoughts would have mattered little to Dudley Patterson or the two other horsemen, Sam Endfield and Charles Cromwell, with whom he was speaking on a late spring day some fifteen years ago. Having spent nearly ten hours sorting steers and branding calves, the horsemen were resting in a grove of juniper trees several miles from their homes at Cibecue. The heat of the afternoon was still intense, and as the men waited for it to subside, their talk was of their trade: the habits and foibles of horses and the dozens of things one needs to keep in mind when working excitable cattle in rough and rocky country. Expert riders all, and intimately familiar with the rugged lands they had explored together for more than forty years, they spoke quietly of such matters, exchanging observations about Dudley's bay mare (strong and quick but reluctant to trot through heavy stands of brush), Sam's roan gelding (gentle and cooperative but apt to bite when hastily bridled), and the spotted maverick bull with curled horns and faulty vision in one eye who could be safely approached from the left side but not from the right. Western Apache shop talk: relaxed, confident, endlessly informative, rising and falling on the soft phonemic tones of the Athapaskan language the horsemen speak with total fluency. As an aspiring speaker of the language and a would-be horseman myself, I am completely absorbed.[7]

A few minutes later, the group beneath the trees is joined by another man on horseback, Talbert Paxton, who is highly regarded as an accomplished roper and a fearless rider in pursuit of bolting cattle. Considerably younger than Dudley Patterson and his companions, Talbert has worked with them many times before, but for the past three weeks, painfully upset over the collapse of a month-long love affair, he has thrown himself into other sorts of activities—such as drinking prodigious quantities of beer, spreading unfounded rumors about the woman who rejected him, and proposing sex to several other women who either laughed in his face or promised to damage his testicles if he took one more step in their direction. Normally restrained and unquestionably intelligent, Talbert had lost control of himself. He had become a nuisance of the first order, an unruly bother and an irritating bore, and the residents of Cibecue were more than a little annoyed.

Nothing is said of this or anything else as Talbert dismounts, tethers his horse to a tree, and seats himself on the ground at a respectable distance from his senior associates. Charles nods him a wordless greeting, Sam does the same, and Dudley announces to no one in particular that it certainly is hot. Talbert remains silent, his eyes fixed intently on the pointed toes of his high-heeled boots. Charles disposes of a well-chewed plug of tobacco, Sam attacks a hangnail with his pocket-knife, and Dudley observes that the grass is certainly dry. A long moment passes before Talbert finally speaks. What he says deals with neither the elevated temperature nor the parched condition of the Cibecue range. In a soft and halting voice he reports that he has been sober for three days and would like to return to work. He adds that he is anxious to get away from the village because people there have been gossiping about him. Worse than that, he says, they have been laughing at him behind his back.

It is a candid and touching moment, and I expect from the smiles that appear on the faces of the senior horsemen that they will respond to Talbert's disclosures with accommodating expressions of empathy and approval. But what happens next—a short sequence of emphatically delivered assertions to which Talbert replies in kind—leaves me confused. My bewilderment stems not from a failure to understand the linguistic meanings of the utterances comprising the interchange; indeed, their overt semantic content is simple and straightforward. What is perplexing is that the utterances arrive as total non sequiturs, as statements I cannot relate to anything that has previously been said or done. Verbal acts without apparent purpose or interactional design, they seem totally unconnected to the social context in which they are occurring, and whatever messages they are intended to convey elude me entirely.

A grinning Dudley speaks first:

Hela! Gizhyaa'itiné dį' nandzaa né.
(So! You've returned from Trail Goes Down Between Two Hills!)

Followed by a brightly animated Charles:

Hela! 'Iłts'ą́ą́ nadaahi niłhiyeeg né.
(So! You got tired walking back and forth!)

Followed by Sam, on the verge of laughter:

Hela! 'Ilizh diłtlii daho'higo bił 'óóhindzii né.
(So! You've smelled enough burning piss!)

Followed by Talbert, who is smiling now himself:

Dit'įį dogosh'įįda. (For a while I couldn't see!)

Followed once more by Dudley:

Dá'andii! Gizhyaa'itiné goyą́ą́go 'ánilą̨' doleeł. 'Iską̨ da łaa
naiłdziig. (Truly! Trail Goes Down Between Two Hills will
make you wise. We'll work together tomorrow.)

The sudden burst of talk ends as abruptly as it began, and silence
again prevails in the shady grove of juniper trees. Nothing more will
be said. Still chuckling, Sam Endfield rises from the ground, walks to
his horse, and swings smoothly into his saddle. Moments later, the
rest of us follow suit. Talbert departs on a trail leading north to the
home of one of his sisters. Sam and Charles and Dudley head north-
west to a small pasture where they keep their extra mounts. I ride
alone toward the trading post at Cibecue, wondering what to have for
supper and trying to make sense of the events I have just witnessed.
But to no avail. What the place named Trail Goes Down Between
Two Hills has to do with too much walking back and forth, burning
urine, and making young men wise are things I do not know. And
why mentioning them succeeded in lifting everyone's spirits, including those of the troubled Talbert Paxton, remains a puzzling question.

June 12, 1982. Three days later, Dudley Patterson would begin to
supply the answer. Short of stature and trim of build, the 54-year-old
horseman presents a handsome figure as he emerges from the small
wooden house where he has lived by himself since the death of his
wife in 1963. Dressed in freshly laundered Levis, a red-checked shirt,
and a cream-colored straw hat, he moves with the grace of a natural
athlete, and it strikes me as he approaches that nothing about him is
superfluous. Just as his actions are instinctually measured and precise,
so is the manner in which he speaks, sings, and dances with friends
and relatives at religious ceremonials. But he is also given to joking
and laughter, and whenever he smiles, which is much of the time, his
angular countenance lights up with an abundance of irrepressible good
will. Expert cattleman, possessor of horse power, dutiful kinsman without peer, no one in Cibecue is more thoroughly liked than Dudley
Patterson. And few are more respected. For along with everything
else, Dudley is known to be wise.

Figure 8 *The great cottonwood tree at Gizhyaa'itiné (Trail Goes Down Between Two Hills).*

It was the merits of wisdom, Dudley informs me over a cup of boiled coffee, that Talbert Paxton needed to be reminded of earlier in the week. But before discussing that, Dudley inquires whether I have lately visited Trail Goes Down Between Two Hills, the place whose name is Gizhyaa'itiné. I tell him I have. Located a few miles north of Cibecue, its Apache name describes it well—two wooded knolls of similar size and shape with a footpath passing between them that descends to a grassy flat on the west bank of Cibecue Creek. And did I notice the big cottonwood tree that stands a few yards back from the stream? I did—a gigantic tree, gnarled and ancient, with one huge limb that dips to touch the ground before twisting upward and reaching toward the sky (fig. 8). And had anyone from Cibecue told me what happened long ago at Trail Goes Down Between Two Hills?

115

No, only that the widow of a man named Blister Boy once planted corn nearby. Had I never heard the stories about Old Man Owl, the one called *Múh hastiin?* No, never. Well then, listen.

> Long ago, right there at that place, there were two beautiful girls. They were sisters. They were talking together.
>
> Then they saw Old Man Owl walking towards them. They knew what he was like. He thought all the time about doing things with women. Then they said, "Let's do something to him."
>
> Then one of those girls went to the top of one of the hills. Her sister went to the top of the other one. As Old Man Owl was walking between them, the first girl called out to him. "Old Man Owl, come here! I want you to rub me between my legs!" He stopped. He got excited! So he started to climb the hill where the girl was sitting.
>
> Then, after Old Man Owl got halfway to the top, the second girl called out to him. "Old Man Owl, I want you to rub me gently between my legs!" He stopped! He got even more excited! So he turned around, walked down the hill, and began to climb the other one.
>
> Then, after he got halfway to the top, the first girl called out to him again in the same way. He stopped! Now he was very excited! So Old Man Owl did the same thing again. He forgot about the second girl, walked down the hill, and began climbing the other one.
>
> It happened that way four times. Old Man Owl went back and forth, back and forth, climbing up and down those hills.
>
> Then those beautiful girls just laughed at him.

Fairly beaming with amusement and delight, Dudley wastes little time beginning a second story about Old Man Owl at Trail Goes Down Between Two Hills.

> Those same two sisters were there again. I don't know why, maybe they went there often to get water.
>
> Then Old Man Owl was walking towards them.
> They decided they would do something to him.

Then one of the girls climbed into the branches of a big cottonwood tree that was growing there. The other girl went to the top of one of those hills.

Then the girl in the tree lifted her skirt and spread her legs slightly apart. She remained motionless as Old Man Owl walked beneath her. Suddenly, he looked up! He had noticed something!

Now he got very excited! "Hmm," he thought, "that tree looks a lot like a woman. I really like the way it looks! I'd best bring it home. I think I'll burn it down." His eyesight was very poor. Old Man Owl was very nearly blind.

Then, having piled some grass at the base of the tree, Old Man Owl set fire to it. The girl in the tree pissed on it and quickly put it out. Old Man Owl looked all around. "Where's that rain coming from?" he said. "I don't see any clouds." So he started another fire at the base of the tree and the girl pissed on it again and quickly put it out. Now he was very confused. The other girl, the one on top of the hill, could hear all that Old Man Owl was saying to himself. She was really laughing!

Then Old Man Owl did the same thing again. He started another fire and the girl in the tree pissed on it and put it out. He was looking around again. "Where's that rain coming from? Where's that rain coming from? I don't see any clouds! There are no clouds anywhere! Something must be wrong!"

Then he tried one more time and the girl in the tree did the same thing again. Old Man Owl stood there shaking his head. "Something must be very wrong!" he said. "I'd better go home." He walked away with his head hanging down.

Then those two beautiful girls joined each other and laughed and laughed. They were really laughing at Old Man Owl.

As Dudley Patterson closes his narrative, he is laughing himself. It is obvious that he relishes the stories of Old Man Owl. Moments later, after pouring us another cup of coffee, he as much as says so—the stories are very old, he has heard them many times, and they always give him pleasure. Besides being humorous, he says, they make him think of the ancestors—the wise ones, he calls them—the people who first told the stories at a time when humans and animals communicated without difficulty. These are thoughts I have heard expressed before, by Dudley and other Apache people living at Cibecue, and I know they are strongly felt. But I have yet to learn how the tales of Old Man Owl played into the episode involving Talbert Paxton. If the point was to inform Talbert that beautiful women can be deceiving, or perhaps should not be trusted, or sometimes enjoy toying with the emotions of unsuspecting men, why hadn't the horsemen just come out and said so? Why had they beat around the bush?

Uncertain of how to ask this question in Apache, I attempt to convey it in English, which Dudley understands with more than fair success. He catches on quickly to the thrust of my query and proceeds to answer it with gratifying thoroughness. Speaking for Charles and Sam as well as himself, he explains that there were several reasons for dealing with Talbert as they did. To have criticized Talbert explicitly—to have told him in so many words that his recent behavior was foolish, offensive, and disruptive—would have been insulting and condescending. As judged from Talbert's apologetic demeanor, he had reached these conclusions himself, and to inform him openly of what he already knew would be to treat him like a child. In addition, because Talbert was unrelated by ties of kinship to either Dudley or Sam, and because he was related only distantly to Charles, none of them possessed the requisite authority to instruct him directly on matters pertaining to his personal life; this was the proper responsibility of his older matrilineal kinsmen. Moreover, the horsemen were fond of Talbert. He was a friendly young man, quiet and congenial, whose undemanding company and propensity for hard work they very much appreciated. Last, and beyond all this, Dudley and his companions wanted Talbert to remember what they would urge upon him by attaching it to something concrete, something fixed and permanent, something he had seen and could go to see again—a place upon the land.

So the horsemen took a circuitous tack—respectful, tactful, and fully in keeping with their status as nonrelatives—with Dudley leading the way. His opening statement to Talbert—"So! You've returned from Trail Goes Down Between Two Hills"—was intended to focus the young man's attention on the place where Old Man Owl encountered the two Apache sisters and to summon thoughts of what transpired there. Dudley's comment was also meant to suggest that Talbert, having acted in certain respects like Old Man Owl himself, would be well-advised to alter his conduct. But in presupposing that Talbert was already aware of this—in announcing that he had *returned* from Trail Goes Down Between Two Hills—Dudley's comment also affirmed his friend's decision to refrain from drinking and resume a normal life. Thus, in a sidelong but deftly pointed way, Dudley was criticizing Talbert's misguided behavior and at the same time commending him for rejecting it as unacceptable.

The ensuing statements by Charles and Sam—"So! You got tired walking back and forth!" and "So! You've smelled enough burning piss!"—sharpened and consolidated these themes, further likening Talbert to Old Man Owl by alluding to key events in the stories that recount his misadventures with the pair of beautiful girls. But these assertions, like Dudley's before them, were couched in the past tense, thereby implying that Talbert's resolve to behave differently in the future was a good and welcome development. The horsemen's strategy must have worked successfully because Talbert responded by tacitly admitting that his actions had indeed resembled those of Old Man Owl; simultaneously, however, he registered his belief that the resemblance had come to an end. In effect, his reply to the horsemen—"For a while I couldn't see!"—conveyed a veiled confession of improper conduct and an implicit declaration not to repeat it. But more was conveyed than this. At one level, Talbert's statement intimated a forcefully simple truth: he had been cold sober for three days and now, having recovered his physical senses, could again see clearly. But at another level, and perhaps more forcefully still, the truth was allegorical. Unlike the myopic Old Man Owl, who never curbed his sexual appetites and remained hopelessly at odds with everyone around him, Talbert was intimating that he had regained his social senses as well. Obliquely but sincerely, he was informing the horsemen that his moral vision had been restored.

Which was just what Dudley Patterson wanted to hear. As Dudley told Talbert before he left to go home, his imaginary visit to Trail

Goes Down Between Two Hills would help make him wise. And maybe it would. With assistance from Old Man Owl and his two alluring tormentors, Talbert had been firmly chastised and generously pardoned, all in the space of a minute in which no one uttered a harsh or demeaning word. In a very real sense, involving at base a vividly animated sense of place, Talbert had been taken back into an important segment of the Cibecue community. He would return to work tomorrow, and that was why the horsemen, including Talbert himself, were still smiling broadly when they left the grove of juniper trees and went their separate ways.

Back at his house in Cibecue, Dudley Patterson drains his cup of coffee and leans forward in his chair. On the ground near his feet a band of red ants is dismantling the corpse of a large grasshopper, and within seconds the intricate patterns of their furious activity have captured his attention. This does not surprise me. I have known Dudley for twelve years and on other occasions have seen him withdraw from social encounters to keep counsel with himself. I also know that he is mightily interested in red ants and holds them in high esteem. I would like to ask him a few more questions, but unless he invites me to do so (and by now, I suspect, he may have had enough) it would be rude to disturb him. He has made it clear that he wants to be left alone.

We sit quietly together for more than ten minutes, smoking cigarettes and enjoying the morning air, and I try to picture the cottonwood tree that towers beside the stream at Trail Goes Down Between Two Hills. I am keenly aware that my perception of the tree has changed. The stories of Old Man Owl make its impressive size seem decidedly less important, and what strikes me as never before is its standing in the Cibecue community as a visible embodiment of myth, a leafy monument to Apache ancestral wisdom. I am also aware that the place-name identifying the tree's location—Gizhyaa'itiné—has taken on a vibrant new dimension. Formerly nothing more than a nicely descriptive toponym, it has acquired the stamp of human events, of consequential happenings, of memorable times in the life of a people. As a result, the name seems suddenly fuller, somehow larger, endowed with added force. Because now, besides evoking images of a piece of local countryside, it calls up thoughts of fabled deeds and the singular cast of actors who there played them out. Gizhyaa'itiné. Repeating the place-name silently to myself, I decide that Dudley Patterson's narratives have transformed its referent from a geographical site into something resembling a theater, a natural stage upon the land (vacant now but with props still fully intact) where significant moral dramas unfolded in the past. Gizhyaa'itiné. In my mind's eye, I can almost see the beautiful Apache sisters . . . really laughing at Old Man Owl.

Still engrossed in his ants, Dudley remains oblivious to the sights and sounds around him—a pair of ravens perched on his tool shed, the distant wailing of a distressed child, a vicious dogfight that erupts without warning in the tall grass behind his house. It is only when his older sister arrives on foot with a dishpan filled with freshly made tortillas that he glances up and sets his thoughts aside. He explains to Ruth Patterson that he has been talking to me about the land and how it can make people wise. "Wisdom," Ruth says firmly in Apache. "It's difficult!" And then, after inviting me to stay and eat with them, she enters Dudley's house to prepare a simple meal. Ruth's remark prompts a surge of ethnographic gloom, forcing me to acknowledge that I know next to nothing about Apache conceptions of wisdom. In what is wisdom thought to consist? How does one detect its presence or absence? How is it acquired? Do persons receive instruction in wisdom or is it something they arrive at, or fail to arrive at, entirely on their own? And why is it, as Ruth had said, that wisdom is "difficult"? If I am to understand something of how places work to make people wise, an arresting idea I find instantly compelling, these are matters I must try to explore.

And who better to explore them with than Dudley Patterson? He is known to be wise—many people have said so—and I have to begin somewhere. So without further ado I put the question to him: "What is wisdom?" Dudley greets my query with a faintly startled look that recedes into a quizzical expression I have not seen before. "It's in these places," he says. "Wisdom sits in places." Hesitant but unenlightened, I present the query again. "Yes, but what is it?" Now it is Dudley's turn to hesitate. Removing his hat, he rests it on his lap and gazes into the distance. As he continues to look away, the suspicion grows that I have offended him, that my question about wisdom has exceeded the limits of propriety and taste. Increasingly apprehensive, I feel all thumbs, clumsy and embarrassed, an impulsive dolt who acted without thinking. What Dudley is feeling I cannot tell, but in less than a minute he rescues the situation and I am much relieved. "Wisdom sits in places," he says again. And then, unbidden, he begins to tell me why.

Long ago, the people moved around all the time. They went everywhere looking for food and watching out for enemies. It was hard for them. They were poor. They were often hungry. The women went out with their daughters to gather acorns, maybe walnuts. They went in search of all kinds of plants. Some man with a rifle and bullets always went with them. He looked out for danger.

Then they got to a good place and camped there. All day they gathered acorns. The women showed their daughters how to do it. Now they stopped working for a little while to eat and drink.

Then one of the women talked to the girls. "Do you see that mountain over there? I want you to look at it. Its name is Dził Ndeezé (Long Mountain). Remember it! Do you know what happened long ago close to that mountain? Well, now I'm going to tell you about it." Then she told them a story about what happened there. After she had finished she said, "Well, now you know what happened at Long Mountain. What I have told you is true. I didn't make it up. I learned it from my grandmother. Look at that mountain and think about it! It will help make you wise."

Then she pointed to another place and did the same way again. "Do you see that spring over there? Look at it! Its name is Dǫ' Bigowąné (Fly's Camp)." Now she told them a story about that place, too. "Think about it," she said. "Someday, after you have grown up, you will be wise," she said. Everywhere they went they did like that. They gave their daughters place-names and stories. "You should think about this," they said.

The same was done with boys. They went hunting for deer with their fathers and uncles. They didn't come home until they had killed many deer. Everyone was happy when they came back. Now they had meat to eat.

Then, when they were out hunting, one of the men would talk to the boys. "Do you see where the trail crosses the wash? Look at it! Its name is Ma' Tẹ́hilizhé (Coyote Pisses In The Water). Something happened there long ago. I'm going to tell you about it." Now he told the story to them. "Don't forget it," he said. "I want you to think about it. Someday it's going to make you wise."

Then they would stop at some other place. "This place is named Tséé Deeschii' Ts'ǫ́sé (Slender Red Rock Ridge). Something happened here, also," he said. He told them that story. "Remember what I have told you," he said.

It was like that. The people who went many places were wise. They knew all about them. They thought about them. I've been all over this country. I went with my grandfather when I was a boy. I also traveled with my uncles. They taught me the names of all these places. They told me stories about all of them. I've thought about all of them for a long time. I still remember everything.

Sitting with my back to Dudley's house, I cannot see that Ruth Patterson has come to the door and is listening to her brother as he speaks of places and wisdom. I sense her presence, however, and when I turn around she is looking at me, her comely face arranged in what I interpret as a sympathetic smile. "It's true," she says in a bright tone of voice. "Everything he says is true. It happened that way to me."

One time—I was a young girl then—I went with my mother to Nadah Nch'íi'é (Bitter Agave). That was in 1931. We went there to roast agave. There were other people with us, quite a few of them. They were all my relatives.

Then we made camp, right below that point at the north end of the mountain. We camped by the spring there. My mother was in charge of everything. She told us what to do.

Then we dug up a lot of agave and brought it back to camp. It was hard work. It was hot. We were young girls then. We weren't yet strong and got tired easily. We really wanted to rest.

Then my mother talked to us. "You should only rest a little while. Don't be lazy. Don't think about getting tired. If you do, you'll get careless and something might happen to you."

Then she told a story. "Maybe you've heard this story before but I'm going to tell it to you anyway." She pointed to that mountain named Túzhį' Yaahigaiyé (Whiteness Spreads Out Descending To Water). "It happened over there," she said to us.

"Long ago, on the east side of that mountain, there were lots of dead oak trees. There was a woman living with her family not far away. 'We're almost out of firewood,' she said to one of her daughters. 'Go up there and bring back some of that oak.'

"Then that girl went up there. She started to gather firewood. It was very hot and she got tired fast. 'I'm getting tired,' she thought. 'I've already got enough firewood. I'll go back home.'

"Then she picked up as much firewood as she could carry. She started walking down to her camp. She got careless. She stepped on a thin flat rock. It looked strong but she forgot she was carrying all that heavy oak. The rock broke when she stepped on it. She stumbled and fell down. She hit her head on the ground. For a while she was unconscious.

"Then she came to and noticed that she was bleeding from cuts on her cheek and chin. She walked unsteadily back to her camp. She told her mother what had happened.

"Then her mother talked to her. 'You acted foolishly but you're going to be all right. You failed to see danger before it happened. You could have fallen off the trail and gotten killed on those sharp rocks below it. You were thinking only of yourself. That's why this happened to you.'"

That's the end of the story. After my mother told it to us, she spoke to us again. "Well, now you know what happened

over there at Whiteness Spreads Out Descending To Water.
That careless girl almost lost her life. Each of you should try to
remember this. Don't forget it. If you remember what
happened over there, it will help make you wise."

Then we went back to work, digging up more of agave.
I got tired again—it was still very hot—but this time I didn't
think about it. I just tried not to be careless.

Nowadays, hardly anyone goes out to get agave. Very few
of us do that anymore. The younger ones are afraid of hard
work. Even so, I've told that story to all my children. I've told
them to remember it.

I thank Ruth for telling me her story. She smiles but her eyes have
filled with tears. Unable to stem the rush of her emotion, she turns
away and goes back inside the house. Dudley is not visibly concerned.
He explains that Ruth is recalling her youth. That was during the
1920s and 1930s when Ruth and her sisters were still unmarried and
worked almost daily under the close supervision of their mother and
two maternal aunts. Back then, Dudley says, Cibecue was different.
There were fewer people and life was less centered on the village itself.
Whole Apache families, including Dudley's own, spent weeks and
months away upon the land—tending cornfields, roasting agave, hunting deer, and journeying to remote cattle camps where they helped
the horsemen build fences and corrals. The families traveled long
distances—old people and children alike, on foot and horseback, through
all kinds of weather, carrying their possessions in heavy canvas packs
over narrow trails that now have all but vanished. It was a hard way
to live—there were times when it got very hard—but the people
were strong and hardly ever complained. They had able leaders
who told them what to do, and despite the hardships involved
they took pleasure in their journeys. And wherever they went they
gave place-names and stories to their children. They wanted their
children to know about the ancestors. They wanted their children to
be wise. Ruth is remembering all of this, Dudley reports, and it makes
her a little sad.

The aging horseman leans back in his chair, crossing a boot over
his knee, and spins the rowel of his spur. *Vrnnnn!* He does this from

time to time when he is thinking serious thoughts. He rolls a cigarette
and lights it with a battered Zippo he has carried for years. *Vrnnn!*
Spinning and smoking at the same time—his thoughts must be serious indeed. Several minutes pass before he speaks. When he does, he
tells me that he has not forgotten my question: "What is wisdom?" He
now intends to address it. He will use his own language, and to help
me understand he will try to keep things simple. He stubs out his
cigarette, rolls and lights another one, and then goes to work. *Vrnnn!*
What follows is poetry and a great deal more about wisdom.

The trail of wisdom—that is what I'm going to talk about.
I'm going to speak as the old people do, as my grandmother
spoke to me when I was still a boy. We were living then at
Ták'eh Godzigé (Rotten Field).

"Do you want a long life?" she said. "Well, you will need
to have wisdom. You will need to think about your own
mind. You will need to work on it. You should start doing
this now. You must make your mind smooth. You must make
your mind steady. You must make your mind resilient.

"Your life is like a trail. You must be watchful as you go.
Wherever you go there is some kind of danger waiting to happen. You must be able to see it before it happens.
You must always be watchful and alert. You must see danger
in your mind before it happens.

"If your mind is not smooth you will fail to see danger.
You will trust your eyes but they will deceive you. You will
be easily tricked and fooled. Then there will be nothing but
trouble for you. You must make your mind smooth.

"If your mind is not resilient you will be easily startled.
You will be easily frightened. You will try to think quickly but
you won't think clearly. You yourself will stand in the way of
your own mind. You yourself will block it. Then there will
be trouble for you. You must make your mind resilient.

"If your mind is not steady you will be easily angered and
upset. You will be arrogant and proud. You will look down
on other people. You will envy them and desire their
possessions. You will speak about them without thinking.

You will complain about them, gossip about them, criticize them. You will lust after their women. People will come to despise you. They will pay someone to use his power on you. They will want to kill you. Then there will be nothing but trouble for you. You must make your mind steady. You must learn to forget about yourself.

"If you make your mind smooth, you will have a long life. Your trail will extend a long way. You will be prepared for danger wherever you go. You will see it in your mind before it happens.

"How will you walk along this trail of wisdom? Well, you will go to many places. You must look at them closely. You must remember all of them. Your relatives will talk to you about them. You must remember everything they tell you. You must think about it, and keep on thinking about it, and keep on thinking about it. You must do this because no one can help you but yourself. If you do this your mind will become smooth. It will become steady and resilient. You will stay away from trouble. You will walk a long way and live a long time.

"Wisdom sits in places. It's like water that never dries up. You need to drink water to stay alive, don't you? Well, you also need to drink from places. You must remember everything about them. You must learn their names. You must remember what happened at them long ago. You must think about it and keep on thinking about it. Then your mind will become smoother and smoother. Then you will see danger before it happens. You will walk a long way and live a long time. You will be wise. People will respect you."

Vrnnn! Rising to his feet without another word, Dudley walks away in the direction of his outhouse. His suspicions were correct; I have had trouble grasping his statement on wisdom. No one from Cibecue has broached this subject with me before, and few have spoken with such eloquence and grace. I am moved by what I have heard but uncertain of what to make of it. And understandably so. Dudley delivered his comments in a distinctive verbal register characterized by conspicuous grammatical parallelism, marked lexical redundancy, and the measured repetition of several dominant metaphors. This resembles the language of Western Apache prayer, and therein lies one of my problems. While the economy of Dudley's speech rendered portions of his statement readily accessible, the metaphors that anchored it—boldly figured, densely compressed, and probably very old—stood well beyond my reach. What, for example, is a "smooth mind"? A "resilient mind"? A "steady mind"? There is another problem as well. I can safely assume that Dudley's account was supported throughout by a covert cultural logic that imbued its claims with validity and truth. Yet it is unclear to me what that logic is. What sort of reasoning supports the assertion that "wisdom sits in places"? Or that "wisdom is like water"? Or that "drinking from places," whatever that is, requires knowledge of place-names and stories of past events? Maybe I have gotten in over my head. Dudley's statement caught me off guard and has left me feeling unmoored. For a split second I imagine myself a small uprooted plant bouncing crazily through the air on a whirlwind made of ancient Apache tropes.

When Dudley returns he is smiling. "Did you understand?" I shake my head. "No, not much." Ruth is also smiling. She is standing in the doorway and looks fully recovered from her bout with nostalgia. She has combed her hair and is sporting the triumphant look of one who knew all along. "I told you!" she says sharply. "It's difficult! Now my brother has made you think too much. Now your brain is really tired! Now you look kind of sick!" Ruth's assessment of my mental and physical condition does little to improve it, and I look to Dudley for help. "I gave you too much at once," he says. "You just need to think about it." Ruth agrees. "That's right! You really need to think about it!" Then she flashes her broadest smile and tells us our food is ready.

But before we go inside Ruth presents us with a suggestion. On the coming weekend, when the horsemen will be off work, Dudley and I will catch up our horses and go for a ride. It might last all day, so we will need to take food. Ruth will provide the fresh tortillas. I will contribute two cans of sardines, a box of Ritz crackers, a slab of longhorn cheese, and four bottles of Barg's root beer. Dudley will take me to different places, teach me their names, and tell me what happened at them long ago. Then, maybe, I will understand something. When we get back home Dudley will speak to me in English—"Boy Keez, I'll see you sometime." Then he will leave me alone to think. In return for these services, he will receive two sacks of flour, two cans of MJB coffee, one sack of sugar, a pail of Crisco, and twenty dollars cash. Now, what about it? For all her endearing qualities—and she has them in abundance—Ruth Patterson is not a person to challenge when her mind is made up, and Dudley, who on prior occasions has pointed this out himself, wastes no time in endorsing her plan. Neither do I. "Good!" says Ruth, whose reputation also embraces an unswerving willingness to capitalize on promising business opportunities whenever they arise. "Good!" she says again. "My brother will help you out. I think you'll really like it."

"Wisdom Sits in Places"

June 15, 1982. Even the most experienced horsemen occasionally get hurt. That is what people say as news of Dudley's mishap circulates through Cibecue. Yesterday, trailing the spotted maverick bull with poor eyesight at the base of a rocky sloped named Tséé Deeschíí'é (Long Red Ridge), Dudley's mare lost her footing, went down hard, and abandoned her rider to walk home with bruised ribs, a dislocated shoulder, and a badly swollen lip. Dudley's first concern was for the welfare of the mare, who returned to her pasture later in the day with nothing more than a few minor scrapes and a glassy look in her eye. This morning, wrapped in a homemade sling that keeps slipping off, Dudley is stiff and sore and in excellent spirits. We sit on the porch of his house as visitors come and go. Ruth has launched a get-well campaign whose main objectives are to accumulate gifts of thick beef broth and to surround her brother with as many children as possible. The children come in shifts to stand beside his chair. He tells them the story of his mishap, and their eyes grow wide with excitement, and he smiles his warmest smile and tells them to be careful around horses and cattle. A little girl steps forward and gives him her orange Popsicle. As I stand to leave, Dudley tells me to come back tomorrow—things will be less busy and we can speak again of matters raised before. I accept his invitation. A small boy approaches his chair and hands him a piece of bubblegum. Dudley is delighted. Ruth's campaign is already a success. Dudley will rejoin the horsemen in less than a week. Our ride together has been postponed.

June 16–19, 1982. For the next four days—drinking coffee, watching ants, and pausing now and then to speak of other things—Dudley and I engaged in a series of conversations about his earlier statement on wisdom and places. At my request, we began by examining some of the statement's linguistic features, focusing attention on the morphology and semantics of its several primary tropes. We then moved on to consider the internal logic of Dudley's account, exploring in some detail the culturally based assumptions that invest its claims with coherence and credible sense. Our discussions dealt with fairly abstract matters, and now and again, when Dudley sensed his pupil was getting muddled, he responded by telling stories that linked his generalizations to illustrative sets of particulars. It soon became apparent that Apache conceptions of wisdom differ markedly from those contained in Western ideologies. More interesting was the discovery that the former are grounded in an informal theory of mind which asserts that wisdom arises from a small set of antecedent conditions. Because these conditions are also qualities of mind, and because they vary from mind to mind, the theory explains why some people are wiser than others.

Stated in general terms, the Apache theory holds that 'wisdom'—*'igoyą'í*—consists in a heightened mental capacity that facilitates the avoidance of harmful events by detecting threatening circumstances when none are apparent.[8] This capacity for prescient thinking is produced and sustained by three mental conditions, described in Apache as *bíni' godilkǫǫh* (smoothness of mind), *bíni' gontł'iz* (resilience of mind), and *bíni' gonłdzil* (steadiness of mind). Because none of these conditions is given at birth, each must be cultivated in a conscientious manner by acquiring relevant bodies of knowledge and applying them critically to the workings of one's mind. Knowledge of places and their cultural significance is crucial in this regard because it illustrates with numerous examples the mental conditions needed for wisdom as well as the practical advantages that wisdom confers on persons who possess it. Contained in stories attributed to the ancestors, knowledge of places thus embodies an unformalized model of *'igoyą́'i* and an authoritative rationale for seeking to attain it. Although some Apache people embrace this knowledge eagerly and commit it to memory in exhaustive detail, others are less successful; and while some are able to apply it productively to their minds, many experience difficulty. Consequently, in any Apache community at any point in time, wisdom is present in varying degrees, and only a few persons are ever completely wise. By virtue of their unusual mental powers, wise men and women are able to foresee disaster, fend off misfortune, and avoid explosive conflicts with other persons. For these and other reasons, they are highly respected and often live to be very old. Likened to water because of its life-sustaining properties, wisdom is viewed first and foremost as an instrument of survival.

Although Western Apaches distinguish clearly between an individual's 'mind' (*bíni'*) and his or her 'brain' (*bitsigha̧a̧*), both are described with a classificatory verb stem (*-ą́ą́*) that designates portable objects whose shape is roundish and compact. However, only *bíni'* can be modified with adjectival constructions beginning with the prefix *go-* (space; area), an instructive bit of morphology which indicates that the mind is conceived of as a region within the brain. This notion is illustrated by the expression *bíni' godilko̧o̧h* (smoothness of mind), which identifies the primary mental condition required for wisdom. When the adjective *dilko̧o̧h* is used without prefixes, it serves to describe the texture of smooth and even surfaces, such as a pane of glass or a piece of varnished wood. But when *dilko̧o̧h* is combined with *go-*, it conveys the sense of "cleared space" or "area free of obstructions," such as an agricultural field from which all vegetation has been carefully removed. This is the sense in which *godilko̧o̧h* is used in the Apache metaphor of the smooth mind. Like cleared plots of ground, smooth minds are unobstructed—uncluttered and unfettered—a quality which permits them to observe and reason with penetrating clarity. Skeptical of outward appearances, smooth minds are able to look through them and beyond them to detect obscured realities and hidden possibilities. Unencumbered by obstacles to insightful thinking, smooth minds "see danger before it happens" and "trouble before it comes." Thus does wisdom flourish.

Mental smoothness is believed by Apaches to be the product of two subsidiary conditions—mental resilience and mental steadiness—which ward off distractions that interfere with calm and focused thought. These distractions are grouped into two broad classes according to whether their sources are external or internal to the individual. 'Resilience of mind' (*bíní' gontł'iz*) combats those of the external variety, while 'steadiness of mind' (*bíní' gonłdzil*) works to eliminate the internal kind. Turning to the first of these expressions, it should be noted that the adjective *ntł'iz* is used alone in the familiar sense of 'hard', thus describing a wide array of objects whose rigid surfaces resist damage and destruction from outside forces. But when *ntł'iz* is combined with the spatial prefix *go-*, the resulting construction, *gontł'iz*, takes on a meaning equivalent to an 'enclosed space that holds its shape'. A tightly woven basket, yielding but strong, is properly described as *gontł'iz*, as is an inflated vinyl ball or a flexible cardboard box that withstands the weight of a child. And so, too, is a resilient human mind. Resistant to the unnerving effects of jarring external events, resilient minds protect their interior spaces by shielding them against outside disruptions that threaten quiescent thinking. Mental smoothness is thereby promoted and preserved. According to Dudley Patterson, fear and alarm present the greatest threats to maintaining mental resilience. Being aware of this, resilient minds guard themselves against shock and consternation, keeping these reactions at bay by centering themselves on what must be done to deal with the problem at hand. Resilient minds do not give in to panic or fall prey to spasms of anxiety or succumb to spells of crippling worry. Largely immune to emotional turbulence, they do not become agitated or disoriented. Even in terrifying circumstances, resilient minds maintain their ability to reason clearly and thus neither "block themselves" nor "stand in their own way."

While resilience of mind contributes to mental smoothness by blunting the effects of external distractions, 'steadiness of mind'—*bíní' gonłdzil*—accomplishes this objective by removing the sources of internal ones. The sense of 'steady' conveyed by the adjective *nłdzil* is that which one associates with a post driven firmly into the ground. The post is stable, it does not wobble, and therefore it is reliable. But the post itself is not responsible for these desirable attributes. As interpreted by Apaches, the post's steadiness is imparted by the hole in which it is lodged, and this is the notion—a 'supportive and accommodating space'—that is evoked by the form *gonłdzil*. Conceived of and described in analogous terms, steady human minds maintain themselves in a manner that ensures their own stability and reliability. This is achieved by relinquishing all thoughts of personal superiority and by eliminating aggressive feelings toward fellow human beings. As a result, steady minds are unhampered by feelings of arrogance or pride, anger or vindictiveness, jealousy or lust—all of which present serious hindrances to calm and measured thinking. Because the essence of mental steadiness lies in a capacity to do away with self-serving emotions that exploit or demean the worth of other people, wise men and women rarely encounter serious interpersonal problems. Free of conceit and hostile ambitions, steady minds "forget about themselves" and conduct their social affairs in harmony and peace.

Except for the mentally impaired, every Apache who enters the world can legitimately aspire to wisdom. Yet none is born with the three conditions of mind required for wisdom to flourish. Cultivating these conditions, a long and uneven process involving much introspection and many disheartening setbacks, has both private and public aspects. On the one hand, it is the responsibility of individuals to critically assess their own minds and prepare them for wisdom by cultivating the qualities of smoothness, resilience, and steadiness. On the other hand, instruction is needed from persons sympathetic to the endeavor who have pursued it themselves with a measure of success. Although instruction may begin at any age, it usually commences when preadolescent children become aware that adult life entails an endless flow of demands that need to be met with special skills and abilities. Young people who have reached this level of understanding are told to be constantly alert to what goes on around them, to remember everything they observe, and to report on anything out of the ordinary. They are also urged to pay close attention to the words and actions of older people whose general demeanor is deemed worthy of emulation. And they are regularly invited to travel, especially in the company of persons who will speak to them about the places they see and visit. It is on these excursions that the relationship between places and wisdom is first made explicit. "Drink from places," Apache boys and girls are told. "Then you can work on your mind."

This view of mental development rests on the premise that knowledge is useful to the extent that it can be swiftly recalled and turned without effort to practical ends. A related premise is that objects whose appearance is unique are more easily recalled than those that look alike. It follows from these assumptions that because places are visually unique (a fact both marked and affirmed by their possession of separate names) they serve as excellent vehicles for recalling useful knowledge. And because the knowledge needed for wisdom is nothing if not useful, the adage that "wisdom sits in places"—'*igoyą́'í goz'ą́ą́ siką́ą́*—is seen to make perfect sense. But there is more to the adage than truth and logical consistency. The verb *siką́ą́* (it sits) incorporates a classificatory stem (-*ką́ą́*) that applies exclusively to rigid containers and their contents. The prototype of this category is a watertight vessel, and thus the adage creates an image of places as durable receptacles and the knowledge required for wisdom as a lasting supply of water resting securely within them. This same image supports the assertions that preparing one's mind for wisdom is akin to a form of drinking and that wisdom, like water, is basic to survival. As Dudley Patterson remarked during one of our conversations, "You can't live long without water and you can't live a long time without wisdom. You need to drink both."

The knowledge on which wisdom depends is gained from observing different places (thus to recall them quickly and clearly), learning their Apache names (thus to identify them in spoken discourse and in song), and reflecting on traditional narratives that underscore the virtues of wisdom by showing what can happen when its facilitating conditions are absent. Drawn from different story genres, these narratives juxtapose a character whose mind is insightfully smooth with one or more characters whose minds are not. Distracted by troubling events or excited at the prospect of achieving selfish gains, characters of the latter type fail to understand the true nature of their situation and perform impulsive acts that bring them and others to the brink of disaster. In sharp contrast, characters of the former type remain calm and unperturbed, grasp the situation for what it really is, and avert misfortune by exercising the clear and wary vision that is the hallmark of wisdom. The social group survives, shaken but whole, and the qualities of mind responsible for its continuation are made clear for all to see. Wisdom has triumphed over stupidity and foolishness, and the difference between them—a difference sometimes as large as life and death itself cannot be ignored.

The two stories that follow were offered by Dudley Patterson to illustrate these themes. The first story deals with serious problems stemming from a lack of mental resilience; the second depicts a near catastrophe brought on by a lack of mental steadiness. In both stories, alarm and confusion run rampant until mental smoothness, accompanied by wisdom, comes to the rescue in the very nick of time.

Long ago, some people went to gather acorns. They camped at Tséé Názt'i'é (Line of Rocks Circles Around). They gathered lots of acorns near Tséé Ditł'ige Naaditiné (Trail Extends Across Scorched Rocks). They almost had enough but they went on anyway. They were going to K'ai Cho 'O'áhá (Big Willow Stands Alone). They stopped on their way where the trail crossed a shallow stream. They had been walking fast and were very thirsty. They wanted to drink. It was hot.

Then their leader said to them, "Don't drink until I tell you to. I want to look around here first." He went off. Their leader was wise. He saw danger in his mind.

Then, as soon as he was gone, a young woman said, "My children are very thirsty. They need to drink. This water looks safe to me. I'm going to drink it." The others agreed with her. "Yes," they said, "we must drink. This water looks good." So they started drinking.

Then, pretty soon, they began to get sick. They got dizzy and began to vomit violently. All of them got sick, including the children. They got sicker. They vomited and vomited. They were scared that they were dying. They were crying out in pain, crying out in fear.

Their leader was the only one who didn't drink. He walked upstream and looked on the ground. There were fresh tracks

by the stream and he saw where Coyote had pissed on a flat
rock that slanted into the water. Drops of Coyote's piss were
still running off the rock into the water.

Then he went back to the people. "Stop!" he told them.
"Don't drink that water! It's no good! Coyote has pissed in it!
That's why all of you are sick."

Then one of those people said, "We didn't know. We were
thirsty. The water looked safe. We were in a hurry and it
didn't look dangerous." Those people trusted their eyes.
They should have waited until their leader had finished
looking around. One of those children nearly died.

That's how that crossing got its name. After that, they called
it Ma' Téhilizhé (Coyote Pisses In The Water).

And again:

Long ago, here at Cibecue, just when the corn was coming up,
an old man saw a black cloud in the sky. It was moving
towards him. He watched the cloud come closer and closer.
It was made up of grasshoppers, a huge swarm of grasshoppers!
Soon they were eating the corn shoots. Ch'iziid! Ch'iziid!
It sounded like that.

Then that old man got worried. "If this is allowed to
continue we will have nothing to eat. All of our medicine men
should work together on this for us." That old man was wise.
He had seen danger in his mind. His mind was smooth.
He knew what had to be done.

Then he spoke to some people and they went to the camp
of a medicine man with strong power. The old man spoke
to him. "Something terrible is happening to us. All of our
medicine men should work together on this for us."

Then the medicine man said to them, "What you say is true
but I will work alone. I will pray and sing. I will help you.
I will bring a great rainstorm to kill these grasshoppers."

Then, that same evening, he started to sing. He sang
throughout the night—but nothing happened! There was no
rain! In the morning, there were no clouds in the sky. The
grasshoppers were still eating the corn. Ch'iziid! Ch'iziid!

Then that medicine man sang alone again. He sang all night. "I will bring lots of heavy rain," he told the people. But still there was nothing! In the morning there were still no clouds in the sky. Ch'iziid! Ch'iziid!

Then another medicine man went to him and said, "We should work together on this. Something very bad is happening. If four of us sing together we can bring heavy rains and destroy these grasshoppers."

Then the first medicine man thought about it. "No," he said. "The people came first to me. I will bring heavy rain if I sing four times alone." So he started to sing again. He sang all night. It was the same as before—nothing happened. Those grasshoppers were still eating the corn. Ch'iziid!

Now the people were very frightened. Some were crying out in fear. They saw what was happening to their corn.

Then that medicine man sang one more time alone—and still there was no rain!

Then four medicine men got together. "That old man was right. We should have worked on this together. Let's get ready, we'll start tonight. That man who sings alone is far too proud. His mind is not smooth. He thinks only of himself."

Then those four medicine men started singing. They sang together throughout the night. They didn't stop to rest! They didn't stop to drink! They kept singing, singing, singing—all through the night.

Then, early in the morning, there was a loud clap of thunder! It started to rain. It rained hard. It rained harder and harder. It rained still harder! It rained for four days and four nights. The people were afraid. They thought their homes might be swept away.

Then it stopped raining. An old woman went outside and looked around. Everywhere there were dead grasshoppers. Their bodies covered the ground. The ground was dark with them. Then that old woman started to walk to her cornfield. To get there she had to cross a wide arroyo. When she got there she saw a long pile of dead grasshoppers reaching from one side to the other. "Grasshoppers piled up across," she said.

Then that old woman knew these four medicine men had worked together well.

Then that old woman went back and told the people what she had seen. "We have very little corn left," they said. "Most of it has been eaten. We will surely get weak from hunger. All of us will suffer because of one proud man."

Afterwards, they called that place Na'ischagi Naadeez'áhá (Grasshoppers Piled Up Across).

While cautionary narratives like these are appreciated by Apaches for their aesthetic merits (their hard-edged terseness, steady forward motion, and mounting suspense can be exploited by gifted storytellers to gripping effect), they are valued primarily as instruments of edification. For persons seeking wisdom, such stories provide time-honored standards for identifying mental flaws and weaknesses, thereby revealing where remedial work is needed and often instilling a desire to perform it. This kind of self-reflexive activity, which is described in Apache as *bíni' naayik'e'iziig* (working on one's mind), is understood to be a drawn-out affair that becomes less and less difficult as it becomes increasingly habitual. For it only stands to reason that the more one scrutinizes one's mind—and the more one acts to improve it by reflecting on narratives that exemplify the conditions necessary for wisdom the greater the likelihood that wisdom will develop. Disciplined mental effort, diligently sustained, will eventually give rise to a permanent state of mind.

Despite this encouraging premise, which for many Apaches is a source of early confidence, the trail of wisdom is known to be fraught with pitfalls. The human mind is a vulnerable space, and protecting it against obstacles that threaten incisive thinking is a formidable task. Life is full of alarming events—deaths, fights, illnesses, frightening dreams, the nefarious doings of ghosts and witches—and the forces of fear are hard to overcome. One tries to surmount them, and later one tries again, but repeated failures take their toll, and attaining the goal of mental resilience begins to look unlikely. Just as difficult is the challenge of ridding one's mind of self-centered thoughts that find expression in harsh and heated ways, antagonizing other people and causing them to retaliate with aggressions of their own. Again one makes determined efforts, and again they fall short, and again one must deal with uncertainty and doubt; mental steadiness joins mental resilience in seeming out of reach. And then there is the never-ending problem of everything else. When one is caught up in the demanding swirl of daily life—caring for children, keeping peace with relatives, trying to get by on very little money—pursuing the trail of wisdom can become just another burden. There is enough to do already without thinking about places and working on one's mind! And so it happens, often with reluctance but also with a welcome sense of relief, that the work is abandoned. At different points on the trail of wisdom Apache men and women simply decide to stop. They have traveled as far as they are able or willing to go. Wisdom, they have learned, is more easily imagined than achieved.

But a handful of persons resolve to persevere. Undaunted by the shortcomings of their minds, they keep striving to refine them—committing to memory more and more cautionary narratives, dwelling on their implications at deeper and deeper levels, and visiting the places with which they are associated as opportunities arise. Little is said of these activities, and progress reports are neither offered nor requested. But progress reports, as Dudley Patterson was quick to point out, are usually unnecessary. As people move forward on the trail of wisdom, their behavior begins to change, and these alterations, which become steadily more apparent as time goes on, can be readily observed by relatives and friends. Most noticeably, inner strides toward mental smoothness are reflected in outer displays of poise and equanimity—signs of nervousness fade, irritability subsides, outbursts of temper decline. There is also to be detected a growing consistency among attitudes adopted, opinions expressed, and judgments proffered—personal points of view, built upon consonant themes, cohere and take definite shape. And there is increasing correspondence between spoken words and subsequent deeds—promises made are promises kept, pledges extended are pledges fulfilled, projects proposed are projects undertaken. As Apache men and women advance farther along the trail of wisdom, their composure continues to deepen. Increasingly quiet and self-possessed, they rarely show signs of fear or alarm. More and more magnanimous, they seldom

get angry or upset. And more than ever they are watchful and obser-
vant. Their minds, resilient and steady at last, are very nearly smooth,
and it shows in obvious ways.

And always these people are thinking—thinking of place-centered
narratives, thinking of the ancestors who first gave them voice, and
thinking of how to apply them to circumstances in their own lives.
Having passed the point where cautionary narratives are mainly useful
for disclosing mental weaknesses, these people now consult the stories as guides for what to do and what not to do in specific situations.
As described by Dudley Patterson, what typically happens is this. Something unusual occurs—an event or a series of events—that is judged to
be similar or analogous to incidents described in one of the stories.
Unless these similarities can be dismissed as superficial, they stimulate
further thought, leading the thinker to treat the story as a possible aid
for planning his or her own course of action. This is accomplished by
picturing in one's mind the exact location where the narrated events
unfolded and imagining oneself as actually taking part in them, always
in the role of a story character who is shown to be wise. If a powerful
sense of identification with that character ensues—if, as some Apaches
put it, thinker and character 'flow swiftly together' (*ndǫǫhgo łeednłį́į́*)—
the experience is taken to confirm that the narrative in question will
be helpful in dealing with the situation at hand.[9] If this sort of identification fails to occur, the narrative is discarded and other stories, potentially more instructive, are consulted in similar fashion. It is
important to understand that wise men and women are able to consult
dozens of cautionary narratives in very short periods of time. Such
concentrated effort is not required of them under ordinary circumstances, but when a crisis appears to be looming they set about it
immediately. Serene and undistracted, they start drinking from places
(in times of emergency they are said to "gulp" from them), and soon
enough, often within minutes, they have seen in their minds what
needs to be done. Wisdom has finally shown its hand. And when it
does, as Dudley Patterson remarked in English the day he cast off his
sling and prepared to rejoin the horsemen, "It's sure pretty good all
right." "Yes," he said thoughtfully. "That's sure pretty good all right."

"Our Ancestors Did That!"

August 10, 1982. But for a gate left carelessly open—and some thirty head of cattle that soon passed through it to lose themselves in a tumbled maze of rock-strewn buttes, meandering arroyos, and dry box canyons—my instructional ride with Dudley Patterson might have proceeded as planned. The day began on a calm and peaceful note. We mounted our horses shortly after dawn, rode out of Cibecue on a trail leading north, and then turned east as the rising sun, a brilliant crimson ball, moved into view above a tree-covered ridge. The morning air was crisp and cool, and all one could hear was the comforting squeak of saddle leather and the hooves of the horses striking softly into the earth. A red-tailed hawk banked on the wind in a vast blue sky.

After lighting a cigarette with his antique Zippo, Dudley broke the silence. "Do you see that ridge over there? We call it Tséé Dotł'izhi Deez'áhá (Turquoise Ridge). My grandmother took her family there when the smallpox came in 1922. So many people died—it was terrible. My grandmother was a medicine woman and knew what to do. She prayed each morning as the sun came up. Day after day she prayed. All of her children survived the sickness.

"And that ravine over there, the one with long white boulders on the far side? Its name is Naagosch'id Tú Hayigeedé (Badger Scoops Up Water). Badger lived there a long time ago, next to a spring where he went to drink. There was no daylight then and the people were having a hard time. Badger and Bear wanted to keep it that way— they liked the darkness—but Coyote outsmarted them. He gambled with them and won daylight for the people. They gambled up ahead where those four round hills sit in a row. Those hills are named Da'iłtąné (The Mounds).

"And way over there, that little clump of trees? We call it T'iis Sikaadé (Grove of Cottonwood Trees). There's a spring there, too. It used to give lots of water but now it's almost dry. Nick Thompson's mother camped there with her parents when she was a young girl. One time an airplane went shooting by. She didn't know what it was. She crawled under a bush and covered her face with her hands. Her body was trembling all over. She stayed under the bush for two days, trembling.

"And that red bluff over there. . . ."

Dudley stops speaking. Two riders have appeared in the distance and are moving toward us at a fast trot. Minutes later, Sam Endfield and Charles Cromwell rein in their mounts and deliver the troubling news. Someone forgot to close the gate near the top of Hayaagokizhé (Spotted Slope), and a large bunch of cattle—cows, calves, and the spotted maverick bull with one bad eye—has moved into the tortuous country behind Kįh Dotł'izhé (Blue House). Judging from their tracks, the cattle crossed over yesterday afternoon. They should be rounded up without delay; otherwise they will scatter over a wider area and make the job more difficult.

Dudley listens quietly, points once with his lips in the direction of Blue House, and off we go to spend the next seven hours searching for wily creatures keenly uninterested in letting themselves be found. A day of quiet learning turns into a punishing game of hide-and-go-seek, and no one finds it the least bit enjoyable. But slowly the work gets done, the open gate is wired shut, and by two o'clock in the afternoon most of the cattle are back where they belong. Only the spotted maverick bull is missing. His tracks disappear at the head of a narrow canyon. Dudley is unconcerned. The bull is strong and smart. He will rejoin the herd when it suits him. One day he will reappear. That is his way.

We have been working in land without water and the heat of the day is hard upon us. Horses and men are edgy with thirst, so instead of returning directly to the village we ride southeast to the nearest accessible point of Cibecue Creek. As it happens, this is Trail Goes Down Between Two Hills, the place where Old Man Owl was shown to be a fool by the two Apache sisters. It is wonderfully cool beside the stream and everyone drinks his fill. Sam Endfield, wearing his pants and hat, decides to go for a dip. Charles Cromwell, whose tender modesties preclude displays of unclad flesh, ambles off behind a thick stand of willow bushes. And Dudley, having twice bathed his face and neck with his handkerchief, sits down beneath the cottonwood tree whose massive lower limb dips to touch the ground. Joining him under the tree, I glance upward into its shade-filled branches, a wholly spontaneous act to which he responds by slapping the ground and bursting into peals of high-pitched laughter. Sam stops splashing in the water, and Charles, looking mildly alarmed, comes stumbling out of the willows trying to button his fly. *What* is going on?

"Our ancestors did that!" Dudley exclaims with undisguised glee. "We all do that, even the women and children. We all look up to see her with her legs spread slightly apart. These places are really very good! Now you've drunk from one! Now you can work on your mind." Still laughing, the weary horseman takes off his sweat-soaked hat and places it on the ground beside him. Then he lies down, cradles his head in the crook of his arm, and goes soundly to sleep. Beneath the ancient cottonwood tree the air is alive with humming insects.

Sensing Places

If nothing else, this truncated tale of congenial Western Apaches, a distinctive brand of wisdom, and a locally infamous cottonwood tree should lend substance to the claim that sense of place—or, as I would prefer to say, *sensing* of place—is a form of cultural activity. Though commonly viewed in different terms—as instinctual need by human ethologists, as beneficial personality component by developmental psychologists, as mechanism of social integration by theoretical sociologists—sense of place, as I have made it out, is neither biological imperative, aid to emotional stability, nor means to group cohesiveness. What it is, as N. Scott Momaday (1976) has suggested, is a kind of imaginative experience, a species of involvement with the natural and social environment, a way of *appropriating* portions of the earth. While this perspective renders sense of place no less challenging to fathom or describe, it demystifies the notion by assigning it to the familiar province of everyday events. Removed from the spectral realm of scholastic reifications—needs, attributes, mechanisms, and the like—sense of place can be seen as a commonplace occurrence, as an ordinary way of engaging one's surroundings and finding them significant. Albert Camus may have said it best. "Sense of place," he wrote, "is not just something that people know and feel, it is something people *do*" (Camus 1955:88; emphasis added). And that realization brings the whole idea rather firmly down to earth, which is plainly, I think, where a sense of place belongs.

A variety of experience, sense of place also represents a culling of experience. It is what has accrued—and never stops accruing—from lives spent sensing places. Vaguely realized most of the time, and rarely brought forth for conscious scrutiny, it surfaces in an attitude of enduring affinity with known localities and the ways of life they sponsor. As such, it is greeted as natural, normal, and, despite the ambivalent feelings it sometimes produces, entirely unremarkable. Experience delivered neat (though not, as I say, always very neatly), sense of place is accepted as a simple fact of life, as a regular aspect of how things are; and if one were tempted to change it, which no one ever is, the effort would certainly fail. It is probable, of course, that your sense of place will center on localities different from mine, just as ours together will center on localities different from Ruth and Dudley Patterson's. But that each of us should be drawn to particular pieces of territory, and for reasons we take to be relatively uncomplicated, is radically expectable. A sense of place, everyone presumes, is everyone's possession.

But sense of place is not possessed by everyone in similar manner or like configuration, and that pervasive fact is part of what makes it interesting. Like all the other "senses" we have invented for mankind (the aesthetic sense, the erotic sense, common sense, etc.), sense of place is inseparable from the ideas that inform it, and just for that reason, as Lawrence Durrell remarked in a letter to a friend, it is "everywhere parochial and everywhere specific" (Durrell 1969:283). Locked within the mental horizons of those who give it life, sense of place issues in a stream of symbolically drawn particulars—the visible particulars of local topographies, the personal particulars of biographical associations, and the notional particulars of socially given systems of thought. It is the latter, of course, that are least available to conscious awareness, and perhaps for this reason writers on place rarely see fit to examine them. Yet it is just these systems of thought that mold and organize the experience itself, and to casually ignore them, as so often happens, is to suppose that matters are much simpler than in fact they really are. You can no more imagine an Apache sense of place without some notion of Old Man Owl, smooth minds, and what occurred at Grasshoppers Piled Up Across than you can fancy a native New Yorker's sense of place without comparable ideas of Woody Allen, contending with subway rush hours, and Central Park on the first warm day of spring. Everything, or almost everything, hinges on the particulars, and because it does, ethnography is essential.[10]

For with any sense of place the pivotal question is not where it comes from, or even how it gets formed, but what, so to speak, it is made with. Like a good pot of stew or a complex musical chord, the character of the thing emerges from the qualities of its ingredients. And while describing that character may prove troublesome indeed (always, it seems, there is something ineffable about it), the elements that compose it can be selectively sampled and separately assessed. Which is what, in a roundabout way, I have tried to do here. Transformative spatial prefixes, disquisitions on wisdom, and cautionary stories of thirst-crazed women and puffed-up medicine men do not "add up" to a Western Apache sense of place. But they can be used to construct one, and thus, taken together, they have something revealing to say about the quality of its tone and the substance of its style. They give us, in short, a sense of the Apache sense, an appreciation of what goes into it, an informed perspective on the angle of its thrust.

And also, I would add, a purchase of sorts on the wellsprings of its force. As vibrantly felt as it is vividly imagined, sense of place asserts itself at varying levels of mental and emotional intensity. Whether it is lived in memory or experienced on the spot, the strength of its impact is commensurate with the richness of its contents, with the range and diversity of symbolic associations that swim within its reach and move it on its course. In its more ordinary moments, as Seamus Heaney (1980) has observed, sense of place stays within the sphere of its own familiar attractions, prompting individuals to dwell on themselves in terms of themselves, as private persons with private lives to ponder. But in its fuller manifestations this separatist stance gives way to thoughts of membership in social groups, of participation in activities that transcend the concerns of particular people, of close involvements with whole communities and their enduring historical traditions. Experienced in this way—as what Heaney (1980:133) terms a "mode of communion with a total way of living"—sense of place may gather unto itself a potent religious force, especially if one considers the root of the word in *religare,* which is "to bind or fasten fast." Fueled by sentiments of inclusion, belonging, and connectedness to the past, sense of place roots individuals in the social and cultural soils from which they have sprung together, holding them there in the grip of a shared identity, a localized version of selfhood.

"Self and mind," Baruch Spinoza (1949:84) wrote, "are essentially one and the same." Assuming this claim to be true, it is hard to conceive of a cultural construct whose bearing on place could be more intimately related to ideas of selfhood than the Western Apache theory of wisdom and its sources. Incorporating places and their meanings into a compact model of mental and social development, the theory of *'igoyą'í* proposes that the most estimable qualities of human minds—keen and unhurried reasoning, resistance to fear and anxiety, and suppression of emotions born of hostility and pride—come into being through extended reflection on symbolic dimensions of the physical environment.[11] Accordingly, features of the Apache landscape, their richly evocative names, and the many tribal narratives that recall their mythical importance are viewed as resources with which determined men and women can modify aspects of themselves, including, most basically, their own ways of thinking. And because changes in ways of thinking are mirrored by changes in patterns of conduct, these same individuals actually can be seen to alter who they are. As Apache men and women set about drinking from places—as they acquire knowledge of their natural surroundings, commit it to permanent memory, and apply it productively to the workings of their minds—they show by their actions that their surroundings live in them. Like their ancestors before them, they display by word and deed that beyond the visible reality of place lies a moral reality which they themselves have come to embody. And whether or not they finally succeed in becoming fully wise, it is this interior landscape—this landscape of the moral imagination—that most deeply influences their vital sense of place, and also, I believe, their unshakable sense of self. For where the likes of Dudley Patterson are concerned—and Sam Endfield, and Charles Cromwell, and the stalwart Talbert Paxton—selfhood and placehood are completely intertwined. Having developed apace together, they are positive expressions of each other, opposite sides of the same rare coin, and their power to "bind and fasten fast" is nothing short of enormous.

At no time, I suspect, is this power more surely felt by Western Apache people than during those sudden flashes of acute intuitive insight that mark the presence of wisdom. In these clairvoyant moments, when wise men and women consult traditional stories and seek to identify with sagacious story characters, their sense of place (and with it, perhaps, their sense of self as well) may reach a kind of zenith. Yet such culminations of mind seem destined to occur with decreasing frequency in times that lie ahead. In communities throughout the Fort Apache Reservation—and Cibecue is prominent among them—fewer and fewer young people are currently embarking on the ancestral trail of wisdom. Caught up with other concerns and reluctant to appear old-fashioned before their watchful peers, they travel less extensively, learn smaller bodies of cautionary narratives, and subscribe with mounting conviction to the imported belief that useful knowledge comes mainly from formal schooling. This is not to imply that young Apaches fail to develop a robust sense of place— on the contrary, they do—but it does get fashioned from new and different materials and points in fresh directions. And that may be all to the good, for as modern tribal leaders point out repeatedly, surviving in the contemporary world requires the acquisition of contemporary skills. It is doubtful, however, that future generations of Apache people will ever devise a more striking way to think about places—and by means of places to think about thinking itself—than the one made known to me by the horseman Dudley Patterson. To him, of course, the Apache theory of wisdom was as familiar as the land he knew so well, as familiar to him as himself. But to me, a peripheral outsider, the model of *'igoyą́'i* was a wonderful discovery, an absorbing cultural form of large and subtle dimensions. And so it has remained, as moving in its way and every bit as gripping as the largely unspoiled countryside from which it draws its strength. My own sense of place, which is not inconsiderable, rests in part upon it.

Time will tell what other cultural constructions await the ethnographer bent on an interest in place. But that such constructions are everywhere to be found—in deserts and savannas, mountains and rain

forests, cities and rural towns—is altogether certain. We should begin
to explore them with all deliberate speed, and not, I would emphasize, solely for the purpose of enlarging our knowledge of particular
social groups. For as surely as place is an elemental existential fact,
sense of place is a universal genre of experience, and therefore, as
more and more work gets done, it may be found to exhibit transcultural
qualities. In this connection, I have already touched on a few possibilities. Ubiquitously accepted as natural, normal, and unexcep-
tional, sense of place is variously trained, variably intense, and,
having grown to mature proportions, stoutly resistant to change.
Its complex affinities are more an expression of community involvement than they are of pure geography, and its social and moral
force may reach sacramental proportions, especially when fused
with prominent elements of personal and ethnic identity. Requir-
ing neither extended analysis nor rational justification, sense of
place rests its case on the unexamined premise that being from
somewhere is always preferable to being from *nowhere*. All of us, it asserts,
are generally better off with a place to call our own. Places, it reminds
us, are really very good.

"That Was His Way."

November 7, 1992. Dudley Patterson joined the ancestors in the
spring of 1983. His wake and funeral were attended by hundreds of
people, some of whom came to Cibecue from many miles away.
Sam Endfield, who no longer speaks of his absent friend and com-
rade, continues to work as a horseman. Charles Cromwell, ham-
pered by arthritis and tired of herding cattle, recently called it quits
at the age of sixty-six. After two or three more drinking sprees,
Talbert Paxton settled down and became a model of sobriety. He
later married a distant cousin and now is the father of three exu-
berant children. Ruth Patterson, invincible as ever, remains firmly
and fully in charge.

On the evening Dudley was buried, not far from a place named
Sǫǫ Ch'íhi'oołé (Flakes Of Mica Float Out), the spotted maverick
bull appeared on the point of a sandstone bluff overlooking the cem-

etery. He stayed there, grazing lightly and occasionally looking down, for the next two days and nights. Then he went away. He has not been seen again. Most people from Cibecue think the bull is dead. Ruth Patterson is not so sure. "No one found his bones," she told me not long ago over a cup of boiled coffee. "The horsemen looked all over and no one found his bones. I think that spotted bull could still be alive. There are many places he could be, many places." A gentle smile crossed her face. "He knew them all, you know. That was his way."[12]

Epilogue

The village of Cibecue has changed in many ways since the day I saw it first in 1959. The valley in which it sits is as lovely as ever—the earth is still as red, towering cottonwood trees still line the creek, and the vaulting sky above them is still immense and deep. The air is crystal clear and the land for miles around—empty, implacable, majestically serene—looks very much the same. But expert horsemen no longer test their skills on herds of half-wild cattle, fewer and fewer cornfields are planted every year, and the road to the highway twelve miles away has twice been widened and paved. Cars and pickups, on which everyone has come to depend, are common. Cibecue has a sawmill now, a handsome school, a supermarket and a fire station, and a well-staffed medical clinic that tends to the needs of burgeoning numbers of children. And there are new houses everywhere: HUD houses, grouped into complexes, which their owners have furnished with wide-screen Tvs, expensive VCRs, and other conveniences of a fully modern sort. The village of Cibecue, open to the world after decades of seclusion, is fast becoming a town.

A visitor to Cibecue today would discover that all of its housing complexes have been given English place-names—fanciful names like Rainbow City, Too Far Away, Desert Storm, and Hollywood—and that each name has a story behind it, amusing and light-hearted, which provides an account of its origin. During the 1991 conflict with Iraq, for example, the complex at Desert Storm was engulfed in a summer squall. At its height, an inspired Apache matron, having proclaimed she was "General Shortstuff," barked military-style orders from the porch of her house to a little boy across the street who refused to get in from the rain. "Go to your tanks, men! Go to your tanks! Get out of Desert Storm!" Thus the name was born. And thus, understandably, the visitor might suppose that the business of naming places is no longer taken seriously by Apaches, that it has fallen by the cultural and linguistic wayside, a casualty of modern times and accelerated exposure to non-Apache ways. But such is not the case. Traditional place-names have recently been made, and will surely be made again, wherever events of pervasive moral significance happen to occur. And no one living in Cibecue doubts for a moment that this is as it should be.

On a late spring day a few years ago, an Apache youth from Cibecue spent the morning fishing on the upper reaches of Cibecue Creek. He caught several trout, which he strung on a stick by their gills and carried to a spot where he planned to fish some more. There he placed his catch on a tiny spit of sand. Suddenly, a mature bald eagle bolted from the sky and sacred bird and impulsive youth fought for the trout lying beside the stream. The eagle won, the young man was badly raked, and a year or so later one of his maternal uncles bestowed a commemorative place-name on the small patch of sand. He named it 'Itsá Ch'iyaa'iłtǫǫłé (Eagle Hurtles Down). Another Apache place came into being that day, and another historical tale—which advises *never* to challenge eagles—now hints tersely at some of the reasons why. Those who "speak with names" have one more name to work with, and those who imagine place-worlds in the future will have one more world to construct. The Western Apache youth, now grown to manhood, is presently in training to become a ceremonial singer. Everyone in Cibecue who has heard him perform comments on the clarity and intention of his voice. Some people say he may one day be wise. The ancestors, no doubt, are watching.

Notes

Preface

1. Readers who might be interested in my first impressions of Cibecue may consult Basso (1990a).
2. Some of these other writings have been collected in Basso (1990b); for a brief general ethnography of Cibecue circa 1965, see Basso (1970).
3. The essays that form the chapters of this book do not appear in the sequence in which they were written, and each has since been modified. "Stalking with Stories" appeared first as a chapter in *Text, Play and Story: The Reconstruction of Self and Society,* edited by Edward Bruner (1984). "Speaking with Names" came next, in 1988, and was published in *Cultural Anthropology.* "Wisdom Sits in Places" was originally prepared for the 1993 School of American Research Advanced Seminar "Place, Expression, and Experience"; a slightly altered version will appear in the School of American Research Advanced Seminar volume *Senses of Place,* edited by Steven Feld and myself. "Quoting the Ancestors," the last of the essays to be written, was completed in 1995 and is published here for the first time. I had toyed with the idea of a book on Western Apache conceptions of place since 1992, but it was not until a year later—thanks in part to conversations with Karen Blu, Dan Frank, Steven Feld, Ronnie Lupe, and Gayle Potter-Basso—that I resolved to proceed in earnest. I hope that those who encouraged the project are pleased with the final result.
4. For informative discussions of why place and space have received little attention in the social sciences, see Agnew (1993), Gregory (1993), and Soja (1989). I am not convinced, as these cultural geographers are, that adopting postmodernist interpretive frameworks will remedy the situation, in part because ethnography—and ethnographic fieldwork—are considered peripheral. One of the aims of the present work is to show, on the contrary, that ethnography (postmodernist or otherwise) is essential, and for reasons that cultural geographers should eagerly endorse.

Chapter 1. Quoting the Ancestors

1. Bohr's comments to Heisenberg are presented on page 45 of Jerome Bruner's *Actual Worlds, Possible Worlds,* published in 1986, and are used by Bruner to launch a discussion of some of the ways in which "products of the mind" are created. Lucid and articulate, Bruner's discussion is well worth attending to, in part because it bears in interesting ways on place-making.

2. My thoughts on world-building generally, and on place-making specifically, have been strongly influenced by the work of Nelson Goodman, especially his *Ways of Worldmaking* (1978), and by the writings of Edward J. Casey, including *Imagining: A Phenomenological Study* (1976), *Remembering: A Phenomenological Study* (1987), and *Getting Back into Place: Toward a Renewed Understanding of the Place-World* (1993). Although my own notion of "place-world" is narrower than Casey's, the two, I believe, are philosophically quite compatible.

3. Place-worlds, of course, are not restricted to constructions of the past; they may also be imagined as pertaining to the future (i.e., "what will happen here?"), as writers of science fiction are well aware.

4. Consistent with the definition proposed by the anthropologist Grenville Goodwin (1942:55), the term "Western Apache" is used to designate "those Apachean peoples living within the present boundaries of the state of Arizona during historic times, with the exception of the Chiricahua Apache and a small band of Apaches, known as the Apache Mansos, who lived in the vicinity of Tucson." Goodwin's *The Social Organization of the Western Apache* (1942), together with his *Myths and Tales of the White Mountain Apache* (1939), provides definitive statements on these people during pre-reservation times.

5. Western Apache place-names are distinguished from otherwise identical expressions by the presence of a phrase-final nominalizing enclitic. The enclitic takes different shapes according to the phonological environment preceding it: -*é* following consonants; -*'é* or -*yé* following all unnasalized vowels except *a;* -*há* following *a;* and -*né* following all nasalized vowels.

6. To my knowledge, there is no word in Western Apache that corresponds exactly to the English word "history" when used in the sense of everything-in-the-past or "the total accumulation of past events" (Concise Oxford English Dictionary, eighth edition, 1990). There is, however, a close equivalent, which is *doo'aniína' 'ágodzaahí,* or 'that which happened long ago'. The expression *ndee binagodi'é* (the people's stories) is used by Apaches in the sense of history-as-it-is-known or "accounts of past events" (ibid.), and this includes narrated place-worlds of the kind presented in this essay.

7. That history is something imagined has recently been acknowledged by John and Jean Comaroff in a collection of their essays entitled *Ethnography and the Historical Imagination* (1992). What is striking about the Comaroffs' approach (and that of a number of other anthropologists whose work resembles theirs) is that it never addresses the question, "*Whose* historical imagination?" As the present essay is intended to show, imagining history is an activity as variable and diverse as the cultural assumptions and materials with which it is accomplished. Ethnographers, to be sure, must worry long and hard about how *they* imagine history (and this the

Comaroffs do with incisive erudition), but they must also try to discern how history gets imagined by the people whom they study (and this the Comeroffs do not do). The trick, in other words, is to look carefully into both, and to allow for the possibility—which the Apache case affirms—that the two may differ in far-reaching ways and perhaps be incompatible and even irreconcilable.

8. I am aware that aspects of this essay touch directly on current characterizations of differences between "oral" and "literate" cultures, particularly as those differences have been formulated by Goody (1977), Goody and Watt (1968), and Ong (1971, 1982). In the case of the Western Apache, whose culture is still predominantly "oral," some of these formulations simply do not apply and are sharply insulting to boot. I am convinced, for example, that statements such as the following are patently false where Apaches are concerned and may thus be of dubious value when applied to other "oral" cultures. From Goody and Watt (1968:34): "[T]he pastness of the past depends upon a historical sensibility that can hardly begin to operate without permanent written records." And from Ong (1982:98): "[The past in most cultures] is not felt as an itemized terrain, peppered with . . . 'facts' or bits of information. It is the domain of the ancestors, a resonant source for renewing awareness of present existence, which is itself not an itemized terrain either." Charles Henry, I believe, would not be pleased to hear this. But neither, alas, do I think he would be surprised.

9. Although Charles Henry was not himself a reader of Western Apache history as written by Anglo-Americans, he had discussed it at length with other Apaches who were, including Morley Cromwell. My own views on its reception among Apache people are based on discussions with Morley and other literate persons from Cibecue. In one of these discussions, involving four individuals whom I knew well, Apache history of the Anglo-American sort was described as 'silent' or 'speechless' (*doo yałti'da*): 'lifeless' (*doo bi'ihi'da*); 'incorrect' (*doo da'áí yeeda*); 'impossible' (*doo bínal'ąąda*); 'overly confident' (*łąągo ya'ołíí*); 'condescending' (*'adiłkąą*); 'hazy' or 'unclear' (*łąągo yaak'os;* literally 'many clouds); 'slow-moving' (*dáłąądágo*); and 'placeless' (*doo nagoz'ąá da;* literally, 'without places). Morley himself, who took a less critical view, observed that written history could be informative (in the sense of bringing new facts to light), and that historical photographs, especially of Apache people and places, were frequently very interesting. He also once observed—and this, I think, is revealing—that Anglo-American historians always seemed to be "working too hard" and to "not have too much fun"; in short, they tended to be relentlessly serious. Works on Apache history by Anglo-American historians with which readers from Cibecue are familiar include Haley (1991), Spicer (1962), Thrapp (1967), and Worcester (1979).

Some of the criticisms just mentioned may be leveled by Apaches against the present work, a nice bit of irony and a source of concern to me. By Apache standards, my book is certainly silent and lifeless, probably slow-moving, and perhaps, in spots, hazy and unclear. I hope it is not regarded as incorrect, overly confident, or condescending. One thing it is not is placeless.

10. Deloria's formulation of spatial conceptions of history, which he opposes to more temporally based conceptions of the past, is presented in his *God Is Red: A Native View of Religion* (1992, second edition). Interested readers should also consult Deloria (1994).

11. Much has been made of late, inside and outside of academic anthropology, of the "sacredness" of American Indian lands, the "spiritual nature" of human relationships with them, and how, given both, Indian people are able to live in a perpetual state of "harmony with nature." At some vague and general level, I suppose this may be true. I also believe (and with this, I know, many Apache people would concur) that matters are much more complex and that outsiders seldom do justice to the subtlety or sophistication of native systems of thought. Consider, for example, that the Western Apache language contains three distinct words for marking *kinds* of "sacredness," that at least three Apache terms could be translated (all of them imprecisely) as meaning "spiritual" or "holy," and that no Apache word comes even close to our own understanding of "nature." In view of such intricacies, I have avoided here the use of contemporary slogans and the simplistic clichés to which they have given rise. If it is true—and it is—that old stereotypes of "Indians" are constantly being replaced by new ones, it seems only prudent to eschew them altogether, or at least to qualify them in careful, informed, and fully local ways.

Chapter 2. Stalking with Stories

1. A prominent figure in Western Apache oral literature, Slim Coyote is appreciated by Apache people for his keen and crafty intelligence, his complex and unpredictable personality, and his penchant for getting himself into difficult situations from which he always manages to extricate himself, usually with humorous and embarrassing results. Short collections of Western Apache Coyote tales may be found in Goddard (1919) and Goodwin (1939).

2. One consequence of this neglect is that few North American Indian groups today possess maps representing the lands that formerly belonged to them. This has become a source of major concern to Indian people, especially in their dealings with state and federal governments. As Vine Deloria, Jr. (personal communication, 1981), has observed, "to name the land was for many Indians a way of claiming it, a way that proved more than adequate until Europeans arrived and started to claim the land for themselves with considerably harsher methods. Now, in litigation over the land, Indian claims can be disputed (and sometimes rejected) because many of the old names that marked tribal boundaries have been forgotten and lost."

3. There has been a recent revival of scholarly interest in American Indian place-names, including excellent studies by Julie Cruikshank (1981, 1990), Eugene Hunn (1991, 1994, 1995), James Kari (1989), James Kari and James Fall (1987), and Alan Wilson and Gene Dennison (1994). See also Klara Kelley and Harris Francis (1994), a study of Navajo places in which, oddly, Navajo place-names are almost entirely absent.

4. Other aspects of the Western Apache place-name system are treated in Basso (1983).

5. Jokes of this type are intended to poke fun at the butt of the joke and at the same time to comment negatively on the interactional practices of Anglo-Americans. An extended discussion of this form of Western Apache humor is presented in Basso (1979).

Chapter 3. Speaking with Names

1. Compatible views on environmental appropriation are expressed in Deloria (1975) and Silko (1986).

2. Silverstein (1976, 1979) argues that a preoccupation with the "semantico-referential" function of language has provided the basis for a uniquely biased Western linguistic ideology in which other functions, especially indexical ones, are accorded secondary importance. In this regard, the views expressed in Tyler (1978, 1984) are also highly instructive.

3. "Emily" and "Louise" are pseudonyms; Lola Machuse, Robert Machuse, and Clifford are not.

4. This verbal exchange was not recorded on tape. I am satisfied, however, as are the Apache persons who participated in the exchange, that the text given here is essentially accurate. What is missing, of course, is information pertaining to prosodic phenomena, but none of the participants could recall anything in this regard that they considered out of the ordinary. Lola Machuse offered the following generalization: "When we talk like that [speaking with names] we just talk soft and slow, so that people know to listen real good."

5. I follow here Silverstein's (1979:195) definition of linguistic ideologies as "any sets of beliefs about language as a rationalization or justification of perceived language structure and use." For an informative discussion of some of the perceptual and cognitive limits that may be inherent in linguistic ideologies, see Silverstein (1981).

6. Refraining from speaking too much has pleasing aesthetic consequences that Apache people from Cibecue value and appreciate. It produces a lean narrative style, concise and somewhat stark, that is notably free of cursory embellishments—a kind of narrative minimalism in which less is held to be more. But it is a narrative style with definite moral underpinnings. Refraining from speaking too much results in effective depictions, and this, Apaches say, is all to the good. But economical speech also shows respect for the ample picturing abilities of other people, and this is better still.

7. The pictorial character of Western Apache place-names is frequently remarked upon when Apache people are asked to compare their own place-names with familiar place-names in English. On such occasions, English names—such as Globe, Show Low, McNary, Phoenix, and others—are regularly found deficient for "not showing what those places look like" or for "not letting you see those places in your mind." Alternatively, Western Apache place-names are consistently praised for "making you see those places like they really are" or for "putting those places in your mind so you can see them after you go away." One Apache from Cibecue put the difference succinctly: "The whiteman's names [are] no good. They don't give pictures to your mind." And a local wit said this: "Apaches don't need Polaroids. We've got good names!"

8. The distinguishing features of traditional narrative genres as articulated by Western Apache people themselves are discussed in chapter 2.

9. Western Apaches readily acknowledge that "speaking with names" is possible only among persons who share knowledge of the same traditional narratives; otherwise, place-names would evoke stories for hearers that were different from those intended by speakers. But this, it seems, is rarely a problem among older people. Most adults living in Cibecue maintain that they are familiar with the same corpus of narratives, and while any narrative is understood to have several versions (and different storytellers have different ways of performing them), there is little confusion as to where events in the narrative are believed to have taken place. Consequently, the place-

name (or names) that anchor a narrative can function reliably to evoke comparable images of ancestral events and corresponding appreciations of ancestral wisdom. Younger Apache people, I was told, are increasingly ignorant of both place-names and traditional narratives, so that for some of them, speaking with names has become difficult or impossible. Although the instance of speaking with names discussed in the present essay features women conversing with women, I have been assured by consultants from Cibecue that the use of this verbal practice has never been, and is not today, restricted to female interlocutors. Apache men, I was informed, employ the practice when speaking to men, and persons of opposite sex may employ it when speaking to each other.

10. Louise, who is distantly related to Emily, is not related to Lola Machuse or Robert Machuse.

11. This view of language and its suitability for an ethnographic approach to the study of discourse has been most fully articulated by Hymes (e.g., 1974). For extended applications of this approach, together with useful theoretical discussion, see Sherzer (1983) and Bauman (1984). Hymes's more recent work (e.g., 1981) is also illustrative in this regard, as are treatments by Bauman (1986), Feld (1982), and Friedrich (1986). Tyler (1978) presents a sweeping philosophical critique of formalism in modern linguistic theory and, on grounds somewhat different from Hymes's, argues persuasively for a more sensitive and sensible approach to the study of language use in its cultural and social contexts.

Chapter 4. Wisdom Sits in Places

1. For information on battles now being waged by indigenous peoples to control ancestral territories, see any recent issue of *Cultural Survival Quarterly.* On efforts by American Indian groups to protect and preserve traditional religious sites, see Vine Deloria's essay "Sacred Lands and Religious Freedom" (1991). On the importance of place as formulated by contemporary poets, sociologists, and philosophers, see the writings of Seamus Heaney (1980) and N. Scott Momaday (1974, 1976); Edward Shils (1981) and Peter Berger, Brigitte Berger, and Hansfried Kellner (1983); and Edward Casey (1976, 1987, 1993), respectively.

2. I would not wish to imply by these remarks that all modern anthropologists are uninterested in cultural constructions of place. On the contrary, exemplary works by Nancy Munn (1973), Clifford Geertz (1980), Steven Feld (1982), Renato Rosaldo (1980), James Weiner (1991), Fred Myers (1986), and others have demonstrated that some ethnographers consider the topic worthy of close attention. The fact remains, however, that place is usually treated as an ancillary phenomenon, as something to deal with descriptively and analytically only when other concerns make this unavoidable. My own point of view, which owes much to the philosophy of Heidegger (1977), Sartre (1965), and Casey (1987), is that place is a crucial element in many forms of social experience and warrants careful ethnographic study in its own right. A collection of essays to be published by the School of American Research Press, Santa Fe, titled *Senses of Place* and edited by Steven Feld and myself, takes what we consider a timely and useful step in this direction. So does *The Anthropology of Landscape,* edited by Eric Hirsch and Michael O'Hanlon, which appeared just as this book was going to press.

3. Heidegger's conception of dwelling proceeds from the fundamental premise, articulated first by Husserl (1958), that all consciousness is consciousness *of* something.

4. Any doubt that this is so is dispelled when one considers that the same locality may be perceived and apprehended in very different ways according to the immediate intentions of those who observe it. Described by some writers as the individual's "current project," these situated aims and purposes guide awareness in specific directions, determining as they do what sorts of knowledge are relevant and applicable, and also, though perhaps less directly, what kinds of sentiment are suitable and appropriate. Thus, a professional oceanographer engrossed in a study of wave mechanics will make of the same secluded cove something quite different than will a rejected suitor who recalls it as the site of a farewell walk on the beach, and this will be true even if oceanographer and suitor are one and the same person.

5. A vivid account of this kind of subject-object conflation is given by Sartre (1965:59–67), who describes in close detail his encounter with a chestnut tree.

6. This approach to ethnographic research is discussed and illustrated at greater length in Basso (1990b).

7. Most of the empirical materials on which this essay is based were recorded on tape, with the prior consent of all Apache parties. Events described under the headings "June 7, 1982" and "August 10, 1982" were documented in writing and later checked for accuracy with Dudley Patterson, Sam Endfield, and Charles Cromwell. "Talbert Paxton" is a pseudonym.

8. Students of Apachean cultures will recognize that conceptions of 'wisdom' (*'igoyą́'i*) bear some resemblance to those of 'supernatural power' (*diiyi'*). According to some consultants from Cibecue, the resemblance is only apparent. Whereas wisdom is within the reach of everyone and results from mental discipline, supernatural power is given to very few people and comes mainly from dreams and visions. It should also be noted that possession of supernatural power does not necessarily imply the presence of wisdom. As Dudley Patterson's upcoming story of the grasshopper plague at Cibecue illustrates clearly, persons with supernatural power sometimes act unwisely.

9. The idea that smooth-minded thinker and wise story character 'flow swiftly together' is nicely consistent with other dimensions of the water imagery that pervades the Apache model of wisdom. That wisdom is likened by Apaches to water—and that using wisdom, or drinking it, is considered basic to survival—seems more than appropriate for a people who have lived for centuries in a dry and demanding climate.

10. It is just for this reason, I believe, that novelists and journalists are often more successful than academic writers in conveying to readers an unfamiliar sense of place. Rather than trying to describe sense of place or attempting somehow to characterize it, novelists and journalists seek to *evoke* it by presenting a host of local details and taking note of their own and others' reactions to them. An implicit aim of this essay is to suggest that similar strategies, suitably modified, can be usefully employed by cultural anthropologists and other social scientists interested in the problem.

11. For any cultural system, what counts as a "place" is an empirical question that must be answered ethnographically. In this essay, I have restricted the notion of place to 'localities on the surface of the earth,' or what Apaches term *goz'ą́ą́ ni'gost'án biká' yó*. A fuller treatment of Apache conceptions of place would explore the fact that places

are known to exist in the sky (*goz'ą́ą́ yáá biyi' yó*), under large bodies of water (*goz'ą́ą́ tú bitłáh yó*), and deep within the earth (*goz'ą́ą́ ni'gost'án bitłáh yó*). That places in these categories are seldom seen by human beings makes them no less real, and certainly no less important, than places on the earth's surface. And in this, of course, the Apaches are not alone. How many of us can volunteer eyewitness accounts of the North Pole, or the thirteenth meridian, or heaven or hell?

12. For several years after Dudley Patterson's untimely death, I sought without success to discuss the subject of wisdom with other members of the Cibecue community. Everyone I approached gave the same reason for resisting my overtures, namely, that he or she could add nothing to what Dudley had already taught me. "But how can you be so sure?" I asked one of my Apache friends in the summer of 1985. "I'm sure," Nick Thompson replied. "You had a good teacher. You know what you're supposed to know. Don't get greedy. It's not wise." On that unequivocal note, I let the matter drop and found other things to do.

References Cited

Agnew, J.

1993   Representing Space: Space, Scale and Culture in Social Science. In *Place, Culture, Representation,* J. Duncan and D. Lay, eds., pp. 251–71. London: Routledge.

Bakhtin, M.

1981   *The Dialogic Imagination: Four Essays by M. M. Bakhtin.* M. Holquist, ed. Austin: University of Texas Press.

Basso, K.

1966   *The Gift of Changing Woman.* Bureau of American Ethnology Bulletin 196. Washington, D.C.: Smithsonian Institution.

1968   The Western Apache Classificatory Verb System: A Semantic Analysis. *Southwestern Journal of Anthropology* 24(3):252–66.

1969   *Western Apache Witchcraft.* Anthropological Papers of the University of Arizona 15. Tucson: University of Arizona Press.

1970   *The Cibecue Apache.* New York: Holt, Rinehart and Winston.

1979   *Portraits of the "Whiteman": Linguistic Play and Cultural Symbols among the Western Apache.* Cambridge: Cambridge University Press.

1983   Western Apache Placename Hierarchies. In *Naming Systems: 1981 Proceedings of the American Ethnological Society,* E. Tooker, ed., pp. 37–46. Washington, D.C.: American Ethnological Society.

1988   'Speaking with Names': Language and Landscape Among the Western Apache. *Cultural Anthropology* 3(2):99–130.

1990a Strong Songs: Excerpts from an Ethnographer's Journal. In *Our Private Lives: Journals, Notebooks and Diaries,* Daniel Halpern, ed., pp. 26–37. New York: Vintage Books.

1990b *Western Apache Language and Culture: Essays in Linguistic Anthropology.* Tucson: University of Arizona Press.

Bauman, R.

1984   *Verbal Art as Performance.* Chicago: Waveland Press.

1986   *Story, Performance, and Event: Contextual Studies of Oral Narrative.* Cambridge: Cambridge University Press.

161

Becker, A.
1982   Beyond Translation: Esthetics and Language Description. In *Contemporary Perceptions of Language: Interdisciplinary Dimensions,* H. Byrnes, ed., pp. 124–137. Washington, D.C.: Georgetown University Press.

Berger, P., B. Berger, and H. Kellner
1983   *The Homeless Mind: Modernization and Consciousness.* New York: Vintage Books.

Boas, F.
1901–1907 *The Eskimo of Baffin Land and Hudson Bay.* Bulletin of the American Museum of Natural History 15. New York.
1934   *Geographical Names of the Kwakiutl Indians.* Columbia University Contributions in Anthropology, no. 20. New York.

Bruner, E., ed.
1984   *Text, Play and Story: The Reconstruction of Self and Society.* Washington, D.C.: American Anthropological Association.

Bruner, J.
1986   *Actual Worlds, Possible Worlds.* Cambridge, Massachusetts: Harvard University Press.

Camus, A.
1955   *Noces suivi de l'eté.* Paris: Editions Gallimard.

Casey, E.
1976   *Imagining: A Phenomenological Study.* Bloomington: Indiana University Press.
1987   *Remembering: A Phenomenological Study.* Bloomington: Indiana University Press.
1993   *Getting Back into Place: Toward a Renewed Understanding of the Place-World.* Bloomington: Indiana University Press.

Chapman, W.
1979   *Preserving the Past.* London: Dent.

Comaroff, J., and J. Comaroff
1992   *Ethnography and the Historical Imagination.* Boulder: Westview Press.

Cruikshank, J.
1981   Legend and Landscapes: Convergence of Oral and Scientific Traditions in the Yukon Territory. *Arctic Anthropology* 18:67–93.
1990   "Getting the Words Right": Perspective on Naming and Places in Athapaskan Oral History. *Arctic Anthropology* 27:52–65.

Csikszentmihalyi, M., and E. Rochberg-Halton
1981   *The Meaning of Things: Domestic Symbols and the Self.* Cambridge: Cambridge University Press.

de Laguna, F.
1972   *Under Mount St. Elias: The History and Culture of the Yakotat Tlingit.* Smithsonian Contributions to Anthropology 7. Washington, D.C.: Smithsonian Institution.

Deloria, V., Jr.
1975   *God Is Red.* New York: Dell.
1991   *Sacred Lands and Religious Freedom.* New York: Association on American Indian Affairs.
1992   *God Is Red: A Native View of Religion,* second edition. Golden, Colorado: North American Press.

1994   Foreword. In *Words of Power: Voices from Indian America,* N. Hill, Jr., ed., pp. v–x. Golden, Colorado: Fulcrum.

Dinesen, I.

1979   *Daguerreotypes and Other Essays.* P. Mitchell and W. Paden, trans. Chicago: University of Chicago Press.

Durrell, L.

1969   *Spirit of Place: Letters and Essays on Travel.* New Haven, Connecticut: Leete's Island Books.

Eliot, T.

1932   *The Sacred Wood.* London: Methuen.

Feld, S.

1982   *Sound and Sentiment: Birds, Weeping, Poetics, and Song in Kaluli Expression.* Philadelphia: University of Pennsylvania Press.

Friedrich, P.

1986   *The Language Parallax: Linguistic Relativism and Poetic Indeterminacy.* Austin: University of Texas Press.

Gallico, P.

1954   *Love of Seven Dolls and Other Stories.* New York: Doubleday.

Geertz, C.

1973   Thick Description: Toward an Interpretive Theory of Culture. In *The Interpretation of Cultures: Selected Essays by Clifford Geertz,* pp. 3–30. New York: Basic Books.

1980   *Negara: The Theatre State in Nineteenth-Century Bali.* Princeton, New Jersey: Princeton University Press.

Goddard, P.

1919   *Myths and Tales from the White Mountain Apache.* Anthropological Publications of the American Museum of Natural History 24. New York.

Goffman, E.

1974   *Frame Analysis: An Essay in the Organization of Experience.* New York: Harper and Row.

Goodman, N.

1978   *Ways of Worldmaking.* Indianapolis, Indiana: Hackett.

Goodwin, G.

1939   *Myths and Tales of the White Mountain Apache.* Memoirs of the American Folklore Society 33.

1942   *The Social Organization of the Western Apache.* Chicago: University of Chicago Press.

Goody, J.

1977   *The Domestication of the Savage Mind.* Cambridge: Cambridge University Press.

Goody, J., and I. Watt

1968   *Literacy in Traditional Societies.* Cambridge: Cambridge University Press.

Greenbie, B.

1981   *Spaces: Dimensions of the Human Landscape.* New Haven, Connecticut: Yale University Press.

Gregory, D.

1993   Interventions in the Historical Geography of Modernity: Social Theory, Spatiality, and the Politics of Representation. In *Place, Culture, Representation,* J. Duncan and D. Lay, eds., pp. 272–313. London: Routledge.

Haley, J.
1991   *Apaches: A History and Culture Portrait*. New York: Doubleday.
Harrington, J.
1916   *The Ethnogeography of the Tewa Indians*. Annual Report of the Bureau of American Ethnology 29. Washington, D.C.
Hartley, L.
1956   *The Go-Between*. London: Hamish Hamilton.
Heaney, S.
1980   The Sense of Place. In *Preoccupations: Selected Prose 1968–1978,* pp. 131–49. London: Faber and Faber.
Heidegger, M.
1977   Building Dwelling Thinking. In *Martin Heidegger: Basic Writings,* D. Krell, ed., pp. 319–39. New York: Harper and Row.
Hirsch, E., and M. O'Hanlon
1995   *The Anthropology of Landscape: Perspectives on Place and Space*. Oxford: Clarendon Press.
Hunn, E.
1991   Native Place Names on the Columbia Plateau. In *A Time of Gathering: Native Heritage in Washington State,* R. K. Wright, ed., pp. 170–77. Seattle: Burke Museum and University of Washington Press.
1994   Place Names, Population Density, and the Magic Number 500. *Current Anthropology* 35:81–85.
1995   Columbia Plateau Indian Place Names: What Can They Teach Us? Unpublished ms. in the author's possession.
Husserl, E.
1958   *Ideas*. London: George Allen and Unwin.
Hymes, D.
1974   *Foundations in Sociolinguistics: An Ethnographic Approach*. Philadelphia: University of Pennsylvania Press.
1981   *In Vain I Tried to Tell You: Essays in Native American Ethnopoetics*. Philadelphia: University of Pennsylvania Press.
Kari, J.
1989   Some Principles of Alaskan Athabaskan Toponymic Knowledge. In *General and Amerindian Ethnolinguistics: In Remembrance of Stanley Newman,* M. R. Kay and H. M. Hoenigswald, eds., pp. 129–49. New York: Mouton de Gruyter.
Kari, J., and J. Fall
1987   *Shem Pete's Alaska: The Territory of the Upper Cook Inlet Dena'ina*. Fairbanks: Alaska Native Center.
Kelley, K., and H. Francis
1994   *Navajo Sacred Places*. Bloomington and Indianapolis: Indiana University Press.
Kluckhohn, C.
1949   *Mirror for Man*. New York: McGraw-Hill.
Labov, W., and D. Fanshel
1977   *Therapeutic Discourse: Psychotherapy as Conversation*. New York: Academic Press.
Lakoff, G., and M. Johnson
1980   *Metaphors We Live By*. Chicago: University of Chicago Press.

Lounsbury, F.
1960 Iroquois Place-names in the Champlain Valley. In *Report of the New York–Vermont Interstate Commission on Lake Champlain Basin,* New York Legislative Document 9, pp. 2166. Albany.

McCullers, C.
1967 *The Heart Is a Lonely Hunter.* Boston: Houghton Mifflin.

Merleau-Ponty, M.
1969 On the Phenomenology of Language. In *Problems in the Philosophy of Language,* T. Dishewsky, ed., pp. 89–101. New York: Holt, Rinehart and Winston.

Momaday, S.
1974 Native American Attitudes to the Environment. In *Seeing with a Native Eye: Essays on Native American Religion,* W. Capps, ed., pp. 79–85. New York: Harper and Row.
1976 *The Names.* Tucson: University of Arizona Press.
1994 Values. In *Words of Power: Voices from Indian America,* N. Hill, Jr., ed., pp. 1. Golden, Colorado: Fulcrum.

Munn, N.
1973 *Walbiri Iconography: Graphic Representation and Cultural Symbolism in a Central Australian Society.* Ithaca, New York: Cornell University Press.

Myers, F.
1986 *Pintupi Country, Pintupi Self: Sentiment, Place, and Politics among Western Desert Aborigines.* Washington, D.C.: Smithsonian Institution Press.

Ong, W.
1971 *Rhetoric, Romance, and Technology.* Ithaca, New York: Cornell University Press.
1982 *Orality and Literacy: The Technologizing of the Word.* London: Methuen.

Radin, P.
1916 *The Winnebago Tribe.* Annual Report of the Bureau of American Ethnology 37. Washington, D.C.

Ricoeur, P.
1979 The Model of the Text: Meaningful Action Considered as a Text. In *Interpretive Social Science: A Reader,* P. Rabinow and W. Sullivan, eds., pp. 92–123. Berkeley: University of California Press.

Rodman, M.
1992 Empowering Place: Multilocality and Multivocality. *American Anthropologist* 94:640–56.

Rosaldo, R.
1980 *Ilongot Headhunting, 1883–1974.* Stanford, California: Stanford University Press.

Sapir, E.
1912 Language and Environment. *American Anthropologist* 14:226–42.

Sartre, J.-P.
1965 *The Philosophy of Jean-Paul Sartre,* R. Cumming, ed. New York: Vintage Books.

Sherzer, J.
1983 *Kuna Ways of Speaking: An Ethnographic Perspective.* Austin: University of Texas Press.

Shils, E.
1981 *Tradition.* Chicago: University of Chicago Press.

Silko, L.

1981 Language and Literature from a Pueblo Indian Perspective. In *Opening up the Canon,* L. Fiedler and H. Baker, trans. and eds., pp. 54–72. Baltimore: Johns Hopkins University Press.

1986 Landscape, History, and the Pueblo Imagination. In *Antaeus, Special Issue: On Nature,* D. Halpern, ed., pp. 85–94. New York: Ecco Press.

Silverstein, M.

1976 Shifters, Linguistic Categories, and Cultural Description. In *Meaning in Anthropology,* K. Basso and H. Selby, eds., pp. 11–53. Albuquerque: University of New Mexico Press.

1979 Language Structure and Linguistic Ideology. In *The Elements: A Parasession on Linguistic Units and Levels,* P. Clyne, W. Hanks, and C. Hofbauer, eds., pp. 193–247. Chicago: University of Chicago Press.

1981 *The Limits of Awareness.* Texas Working Papers in Sociolinguistics 84. Austin: Southwest Educational Development Laboratory.

Soja, E.

1989 *Postmodern Geographies: The Reassertion of Space in Critical Social Theory.* London: Verso.

Spicer, E.

1962 *Cycles of Conquest: The Impact of Spain, Mexico, and the United States on the Indians of the Southwest, 1533–1960.* Tucson: University of Arizona Press.

Spinoza, B.

1949 *Ethics,* J. Gutman, ed. New York: Hafner.

Thrapp, D.

1967 *The Conquest of Apachería.* Norman: University of Oklahoma Press.

Trager, G.

1968 Whorf, Benjamin L. In *International Encyclopedia of the Social Sciences,* vol. 16, D. Sills, ed., pp. 536–37. New York: Cromwell Collier and MacMillan.

Tyler, S.

1978 *The Said and the Unsaid: Mind, Meaning, and Culture.* New York: Academic Press.

1984 The Vision in the Quest, or What the Mind's Eye Sees. *Journal of Anthropological Research* 40:23–40.

Weiner, J.

1991 *The Empty Space: Poetry, Space, and Being among the Foi of Papua New Guinea.* Bloomington: University of Indiana Press.

Wilson, A., and G. Dennison

1994 *Navajo Place Names: An Observer's Guide.* Guilford, Connecticut: Jeffrey Norton.

Worcester, D.

1979 *The Apaches: Eagles of the Southwest.* Norman: University of Oklahoma Press.

Index